GOT
YOUR
BACK

GOT

THE LIFE OF A
BODYGUARD IN THE

YOUR

HARDCORE WORLD
OF GANGSTA RAP

BACK

FRANK ALEXANDER
WITH HEIDI SIEGMUND CUDA

ST. MARTIN'S PRESS
NEW YORK

GOT YOUR BACK: THE LIFE OF A BODYGUARD IN THE HARDCORE
WORLD OF GANGSTA RAP. Copyright © 1998 by Frank Alexander and
Heidi Siegmund Cuda. All rights reserved. Printed in the United States
of America. No part of this book may be used or reproduced in any
manner whatsoever without written permission except in the case of brief
quotations embodied in critical articles or reviews. For information, address St. Martin's Press, 175 Fifth Avenue, New York, NY 10010.

Design by *Bryanna Millis*

Library of Congress Cataloging-in-Publication Data

Alexander, Frank.
    Got your back: the life of a bodyguard in the hardcore world of
gansta rap / Frank Alexander with Heidi Siegmund Cuda.
        p.   cm.
    ISBN 0-312-18111-6
    1. Shakur, Tupac, 1971–1996.   2. Rap musicians—United
States—Biography.   I. Cuda, Heidi Siegmund.   II. Title.
ML420.S529A8   1998
782.42164'9'0922—dc21
[B]   97-46984
                                                              CIP
                                                               MN

First Edition: July 1998

10   9   8   7   6   5   4   3   2   1

Books are available in quantity for promotional or premium use. Write
to Director of Special Sales, St. Martin's Press, 175 Fifth Avenue, New
York, NY 10010, for information on discounts and terms, or call toll-
free (800) 221-7945. In New York, call (212) 674-5151 (ext. 645).

*I dedicate this book in memory of
Tupac Amaru Shakur and Yak Fula*

CONTENTS

INTRODUCTION ix

PART ONE: MY LIFE
CHAPTER ONE: Chicago, Illinois—Robert Taylor Projects 3
CHAPTER TWO: A Few Good Men 12
CHAPTER THREE: Kash, Prince of Ears 19

PART TWO: DEATH ROW
CHAPTER FOUR: Wrightway Security 29
CHAPTER FIVE: Snoop and Tha Dogg Pound 35
CHAPTER SIX: Dr. Dre 46

PART THREE: TUPAC SHAKUR
CHAPTER SEVEN: Pac 53
CHAPTER EIGHT: The Chosen One 58
CHAPTER NINE: Death Around the Corner—Gettin' Paid 63

PART FOUR: THUG LIFE
CHAPTER TEN: Candy 73
CHAPTER ELEVEN: Hoochies and Groupies 80
CHAPTER TWELVE: Famous Sexual Encounters 92
CHAPTER THIRTEEN: Italy 103
CHAPTER FOURTEEN: Fight Nights 123
CHAPTER FIFTEEN: Hit 'Em Up 138
CHAPTER SIXTEEN: Lemika 141

PART FIVE: DEATH IN VEGAS

CHAPTER SEVENTEEN: Las Vegas, Nevada, September 7,
    1996   149
CHAPTER EIGHTEEN: Scapegoat   162
CHAPTER NINETEEN: Me Against the World   173
CHAPTER TWENTY: Death in Los Angeles: The Shooting of
    Biggie Smalls   184

PART SIX: THE AFTERMATH

CHAPTER TWENTY-ONE: I Ain't Mad Atcha: To Suge
    Knight and The Death Row Family   191
CHAPTER TWENTY-TWO: To Pac   198
CHAPTER TWENTY-THREE: Eulogy   214

INTRODUCTION

On January 17, 1998, I was baptized for the first time. This book was written before I was saved.

In 1995, I began working as a bodyguard for the artists of Death Row Records. In 1996, I became Tupac Shakur's main bodyguard and was on duty the night he was shot in Las Vegas. Ever since I began working on this book project, the first words out of a lot of people's mouths are, "Aren't you afraid?"

The fear they're imagining I should have, is fear of retaliation for telling the story of Tupac's last year, his relationship with Suge Knight, and my relationship with them. The fact is, I'm telling a much bigger story than that. I'm telling the story of what it's like to grow up in America's ghettos, the tricks it plays on your heart and how you become a man.

Why should I be scared to tell this story? This book is all about the truth, which means it's not about good guys and bad guys, it's about people, surviving. You decide who the villains are.

Tupac used to say, "My only fear of death is reincarnation." He sleeps with angels now, while we're still here on earth.

—*Frank Alexander*

PART ONE

MY LIFE

CHAPTER ONE

CHICAGO, ILLINOIS—ROBERT TAYLOR PROJECTS

I was born in the city of Chicago thirty-eight years ago, one of nine kids, the fifth child, and one of seven sons. The first place I remember anything about was the projects. The projects were a real hard, fucked-up place for a kid to be living. I grew up on the fifteenth floor of a tenement located on Chicago's South Side, at the intersection of Federal and State Streets. The building I lived in was part of the Robert Taylor Projects; till this day, I don't know who he is but he must be one rich muthafucka because the projects were huge. Each building had three wings, and they were built from cinder bricks. The inside looked just like the outside, except maybe the walls were painted.

Walking to school was like taking your life in your hands, every day. Nothing but black people were living there, but we all came from projects with different-colored paint, so we fought over colors. Our set was white, and I had to walk through the red building projects to get to school. There was no way around it. We got into fights on our way to school every morning, because the white projects and the red projects were at war.

My homeboy, Larry Condiff, remembers the playground wasn't so safe, either. "The projects in Chicago were notorious," says Larry. "I can remember back as a kid, playing in the playground and spinning around on the merry-go-round. Somebody threw another person off of the sixteenth floor, right in the center of the merry-go-round. Everybody on the merry-go-round was just splattered with blood, including me. I was seven or eight years old."

Larry's nickname as a kid was Short Cut, because he knew every short cut on the South Side of Chicago. I used to roll with his older brother Sammy, but we all grew up together. Larry and I hooked up again two years ago, because we both ended up working for Wrightway Security, the company that hired bodyguards for Death Row.

Every now and then we reminisce about our neighborhood, but it's so fucked up because all our friends from childhood are either dead or in prison. Larry and I managed to escape the South Side. I got out because I joined the military. Larry got out because he did time.

When we were kids, though, it was wartime in Chicago, and we were the soldiers.

When I was about ten, Martin Luther King, Jr., got assassinated, and I watched Chicago burn. After the riots, I remember driving through the streets with my parents, and the National Guard was everywhere, with their guns and their uniforms. We moved through the streets so slowly it was like we were in slow motion. Everywhere I looked, I saw buildings burning. I can't recall whether I was sad or not. All I know, is I hated those muthafuckin' projects. There were too many people living on top of each other.

People would come up and steal the shoes off your feet. They'd just say to you, "Gimme those shoes." If they were bigger than you, you'd take them off and give 'em up. I remember getting robbed all the time, when I would go to the store across the street for my mom.

My real dad was living in the South, and I'd visit him sometimes, but he didn't treat me one way or the other. Never got a birthday card or a present from him. It was my stepfather, Perry Means, who took care of me. He had sixteen kids, three with my mother, and they met when I was two years old. Perry and my mom were married for twenty-seven years, up until his death in February 1985. His father owned a cab company called Max Livery, and he and my mother ran the company and eventually inherited it. They worked long hours, and I was left at home a lot, with all the kids, helping to raise them.

Greta Smith, my mother, is a piece of work. I love my mother dearly, but back then, we got into it all the time. She's a survivor, she's already outlived three of her husbands, and she taught me how to survive, too. As a kid, though, I didn't appreciate it.

Put it like this, when she speaks, you listen. She'll call you a bitch and muthafucka before you can get a word out. She's no joke.

It wasn't easy being this woman's son. She cursed at me because I hated takin' her dog out. She used to wake me up at three-thirty in the morning to walk her poodle. It was a little toy poodle—B. J. was that muthafucka's name. We lived on the fifteenth floor and the elevators would get stuck all the time; you could end up waiting there for an hour or till the next day because they never worked right. Rather than chance it, I'd walk down fifteen flights of stairs to take this dog out. If she came home from work and the dog had pissed in the house, she'd whip my ass and make me go walk that damn dog. In the snow, to boot.

The projects were a place that fueled rebellion, and I started getting really rebellious. I remember her chasing me around the apartment with a broom one night. She went to hit me, I raised my arm up, and the broom broke. She never hit me again.

At the time, I thought I was Bruce Lee anyhow. I'd started taking martial arts from a family that lived at the other end of the hallway. This dude used to teach karate in the laundry room on our floor. I learned how to punch and kick. I'm thinking I'm Mr. Karate and shit. The floor crazies lived next door to us. They were a family that was just really nutty, and I got into a fight with one of the kids. I had my whole Bruce Lee thing going, but this kid managed to stab me in my leg with a big, long-ass pair of black scissors. I still got the scar today. My play cousin, Darryl Porter, beat the shit out of him after that.

One day, Greta decided she'd had enough. It was time to move out of the projects and into a house. I didn't even know what a "house" was. We moved into an area called Jeffrey Manor, on the other side of Stoney Island. Our house was similar to what you call a town house, it shared a wall with a neighbor and the neighborhood was lined with houses and trees. I'd never seen a nicer street in my life.

Larry's family moved out of the projects into the Manor about two years after we did, and we became neighbors again.

"We actually thought we'd moved to heaven," says Larry. "When we moved out of the projects into the Jeffrey Manor, it was like moving from Watts to Beverly Hills."

As the years went on, the neighborhood started changing. It wasn't long before it became just as infamous as the projects. Till this day, though, I remember how pretty it was when we first moved there.

One of the big problems was, the whole neighborhood was filled with too many mouths to feed and too few dads. Larry had five brothers, and his mom was working two to three jobs to try to support the family. We all looked out for each other, though. Greta became a surrogate mom to Larry. No matter how many kids my mom had, she always made room for more.

"It was different back then," says Larry. "People in black neighborhoods now don't give a damn about each other. In our neighborhoods, when we moved from the projects out to the Jeffrey Manor, none of us ever went hungry. Whoever's house you were at, you were more than welcome to eat." If my family didn't have food, we could go to Larry's house. If Larry's family didn't have food, they could come to our house.

But even as kids, we were determined to start making our own money. Me and Larry got jobs working for milk trucks, delivering milk and juice. I started working for a dry cleaner's. By the time Larry was fourteen, he worked at a funeral home, dressing bodies and putting them in coffins. After that, he stopped fearing death and started becoming a pretty dangerous kid.

I wasn't much better when I was that age. Somewhere around sixth or seventh grade, I started to adopt an "I don't give a fuck" attitude. School was nonexistent for the next two years. I don't even remember going to school in junior high. I started rolling with a crew, and we were always in trouble. I became a terrorizer.

I had two friends who were my age, Johnny Brown, and this dude named Richard. In one year, we had twenty teachers. The three of us ran them out. I was just bad, and we all fed off each other. We used to jump out the window, right in the middle of class, go down to the candy store or go hang out somewhere. Then we'd climb back in through the windows and the teacher wouldn't do shit, they wouldn't say shit, they wouldn't even write us up. We used to egg their cars, whatever we could do to fuck with them.

Back before we had real guns, we used to make our own, called "zip guns." We'd break an antenna off of a car, pull it apart, then file the base of the antenna—the thickest and longest part—until we got a little hole in it. Then we'd bend it up, and with some shear cutters, cut a small hole that's big enough for a .22 bullet. With a block of wood, some electrical tape, a door hinge, and some rubber bands, and I can still make that gun in five minutes. We also used to make pipe bombs with Vaseline and matches.

We were Robbin' Hoodlums, straight up. We used to break into trains and steal whatever was on board. One time, we stole a shipment of Planter's Peanuts and sardines and gave them to everybody in the neighborhood. The train detectives tried to shoot at us with pepper guns, which were shotguns loaded with pepper. They wouldn't kill you but they'd mess you up.

One Fourth of July, we stole TNT; it's a wonder we didn't kill ourselves. It's funny to look back and remember we got our kicks by lighting off dynamite.

I also had this cousin named Michael. He wasn't my real cousin, but he moved into the neighborhood at the same time I did, and we sort of adopted each other. Even back then, he was a con and a master minder. He's in jail now, his life stayed on that path, but we pulled all kinds of pranks together.

Larry became a hardcore gangbanger, one of Chicago's Black Stone Rangers, before leaving that set for another one of the South Side gangs. He'd hooked up with this neighborhood cop named Hector Barnes. Hector owned four gas stations, two lounges, apartment buildings, and a liquor store. He needed someone to help keep things cool with the neighborhood.

"Hector was a notorious police officer," says Larry. "He was well known within the police department for kicking ass."

Larry took it really hard when Hector was murdered in 1978. Larry was only seventeen, and Hector was the closest thing Larry had to a father. "He took a lot of time with me, and he never treated me like a child," says Larry. "He always demanded I be a man, regardless of the situation, and I learned to always carry myself like a man. He was the one who taught me not to take shit from anybody, and I still don't."

I can attest to that. When Death Row started punking me after Tupac's murder, Larry stood up for me. He even quit his job with Wrightway. It's difficult to understand what it means to be a "homeboy," unless you've grown up the way we grew up. Larry's my homeboy.

To go to Bowen High School in the district I was from, meant you had to go east. So now, even though I wasn't fighting my way through the red projects anymore, I had to fight against the Mexicans who lived on the East Side. Hardcore Mexicans.

They didn't want blacks going to their school or hanging out on their turf. I'll never forget rioting and fighting in high school, just to go home.

It was always worst on the first and the last day of school. The blacks and the Mexicans fought all the time, it never stopped. The shit was so bad. I remember running down the hallway with one of my partners and grabbing a wall locker and pulling it off the wall and watching it fall behind us. We took off as fast as we could, trying to get out of school and out of the fuckin' neighborhood.

Bowen High School wasn't near my hood, but every summer, we wanted to go to Trumble Park, or "Trouble Park," as it was nicknamed. It was at 103rd Street and it was a Mexican hangout. It was in the middle of some East Side projects but they weren't like the tenements I grew up in. The buildings were smaller and lower but it was still projects style. This park belonged to the same Mexicans we fought in school. Belonged to . . . that's funny, because it didn't belong to no one. It was a public park, and just in the projects, we were fighting over shit that wasn't ours.

The winter is so cold in Chicago, people go wild in the summer, just waiting to go outdoors. If you're a kid, all you can think about is summer vacation. Every summer, when school was over, everybody wanted to go to Trumble Park to go swimming. Needless to say, the Mexicans didn't want us there. We used to show up to go swimming, and we'd get attacked by these muthafuckas with baseball bats, chains, pipes, all kinda shit. You'd be coming out of the pool, go into the locker room, and they'd just come out from everywhere, and be pouncing on your ass, literally trying to kill you.

I didn't know where that kind of hatred was coming from. Every time me, Johnny Brown, and Rich would be getting ready to leave the pool, the Mexicans were waiting for us by the fence. One time, it was toward the end of summer and I was probably about fifteen years old. They were waiting for us like a pack of lions looking for prey.

When I was sixteen, I started carrying a Bible wherever I went, me and another one of my play cousins Darryl—the guy who beat the shit out of the crazy kid who stabbed me with scissors in the projects. Me and Darryl never went anywhere without a Bible. We used to stop people on the street or on a bus and try to talk to them about The Word.

I look back now and I can see this kid reaching for a way out. The kid was me.

Darryl never made it out. I don't know exactly what happened to him, but people say he got into some bad shit. Johnny Brown's dead now. He got killed in Trumble Park. I heard Richard died of an overdose after someone turned him on to drugs.

Sammy, Larry's older brother, was my age, and we used to exchange clothes all the time. Me and Sammy prided ourselves on dressing sharp. One day, I borrowed a coat of his, and wore it to school. It was a sweetass leather coat with a blue fur collar, Larry calls it an "ol' Super Fly coat," and it pretty much was. We were doing the Mack thing; we used to have walking canes and the whole bit. "On a bus," adds Larry. This was before we all had wheels.

Some members of the Black Stone Rangers, the biggest gang on the South Side, stepped to me at school. I was with my friend Bridget, and we were just leaving for home when they saw Sammy's coat and decided they liked it. These guys took it right off of me. I was probably about sixteen, and there was nothing I could do about it.

Sammy just completely freaked out over this coat being stolen, and I ended up getting it back for him the next day. This dude named Cookie Man was dating Bridget at the time, she lived across the street from Larry and Sammy, and she told him what happened. The gang that had taken the coat was part of Cookie Man's gang, and since he liked Bridget, and Bridget happened to be with me when it happened, he got it back for us.

Everything in the ghetto was about power and survival. As I look back, I can see what was going on in my neighborhood, but when you're living it, you can't see the tricks being played on you.

Just the perception of having more than the next guy, puts you at war. I was going out with a woman and this dude, Mackie and his brother Manford, were jealous of me. They spread the word they were going to beat me up. I was working at a drugstore at the time, and when I was walking home one day, they jumped me. There was ice and snow everywhere, and they, along with some of their friends, beat me up.

I didn't try to retaliate, I just let it blow over. My girlfriend's sister heard about it, though, because she was going out with Manford. She stepped to him and said, "Why'd you jump Frank? He's just a kid." Manford was a senior in high school, and I was probably a freshman or sophomore.

Time went by and everything was forgotten, or so I thought. One day, me and another one of my homeboys, a guy named Larry Henry, were driving down a neighborhood street, and we came to a stoplight. The brothers saw us before we saw them. They were piled into a truck in front of me and before I recognized who they were, they started throwing shit at my car, hitting my front windshield with bricks and rocks.

I backed up a little bit, and they sped off.

I went home, and I got my gun, a snub-nosed .38-caliber. I stuck it up under the seat and I drove to their neighborhood. As soon as we spotted them, we jumped out of the car and stating throwing down, fist to fist.

Mackie ran to his house and came back with a pair of hedge clippers. He started coming at me with the shears and I ran to my car, pulled out my gun, turned around, and starting shooting at him. I shot of a couple of rounds and everybody starting running in all directions.

The girl I was going out with was coming around the corner with her sister and her mother, and they saw me with the gun in my hand. They ran in the house, and called the police while I hopped in my car and went back home.

Me and Larry Henry got back to my house and sat on the porch, like nothing had happened. Within minutes, the police start scoping the neighborhood. Nothing ever happened and they never came after me.

Mackie had a change of attitude, though. He came over to my house about a week later and apologized for everything. He was kissing my ass, but it was done and over with. I wasn't trying to continue anything; they were the ones who started it in the first place.

As I got a little bit older, I started getting tired of this fuckin' city. I hadn't quite gotten to the point where I knew there were other ways to live, but I was willing to take a chance. I couldn't imagine shit being more fucked-up than it was where I lived in Chicago.

By the time you're a teenager, you've seen everything. I'd seen all the drugs, I'd seen all the gambling. My family all gambled. My uncle is a professional gambler, he never worked a day in his life. They had crap games in the basement of my house all the time. The house got paid and we were the house. It was something people just did. The same shit everybody sees today—prostitution, alcoholism—I saw it in my neighborhood. I dealt with it in my family—it's how I came up. Luckily for me, I had a stepbrother, Adrian Means, who was watching me go through this drama, and he came and took me out of it.

I know now if I stayed in Chicago, like my friends, I would probably be dead or in jail. Adrian came and got me around the time I was a high-school junior, and moved me to Harvey, Illinois. He knew what I was going through in the city, because he'd escaped also. He worked hard and saved up enough money to buy a Texaco station in Harvey, a suburb about forty minutes outside of the city.

It was different living in Harvey. It was cool. It was the first time in my life I started to get a feel for who I was and what I liked, and one of the things I discovered was, I liked women. I went from being a kid to a man overnight.

My brother hooked me up with a car, a '64 Chevy Impala. It was white and it was ugly. He had a friend with a body shop who said to him one night, "Give me the car." I thought my brother was giving him the car, I didn't know what was up. The next day, his friend comes back with my Impala, and the car was orange. It was the prettiest orange you've ever seen. The car was so cool.

I had a job, working for Adrian at the gas station, and I transferred to a high school called Thornton. I started to get into sports. I got on the football team, and I fell in love for the first time. Compared to my home-boys, I had everything.

It ended up different for Larry. By the time he was eighteen, he was one of seven guys running southeast Chicago's underground drug network. He'd become a Chicago gangsta. "Compared to L.A., Chicago's like college and L.A.'s kindergarten," he says. "All the dirt you do is specific. No one ever got hurt randomly. My family never even knew my business until it hit the newspapers."

Larry ended up doing three and a half years time in the Cook County jail. That's when he decided he would never give anyone the opportunity to control his life again. I was more fortunate, because I'd gotten out before adulthood. Still, I couldn't live off my brother forever, and I had no plans to move back to the Manor. Nothing on this earth was gonna take me back there.

CHAPTER TWO

A FEW GOOD MEN

Back in 1978, the Marine Corps was still made up of some tough, badass muthafuckas. Their reputation from the Vietnam War preceded them. The Corps was known for its strength, its killing, and its aggression. When it comes to combat, it's the most powerful unit of the armed forces. I decided to join when I was eighteen. I entered in January 1978, and turned nineteen in boot camp.

My first station was in Okinawa, Japan. It was a total escape from the world. I didn't know where I was. It was a big, big culture shock because I'd never seen anything in my life but black. I started meeting people of all races, all different colors, and we were all down together. I started seeing the world differently for the first time. Up till then, I'd only known Chicago, and that's how I thought the world was, just fucked-up everywhere.

I started taking classes, and I got my high-school diploma. The rest of my school life had been all messed up, but the Marines gave me a shot to finish my education. I got my original high-school diploma.

The island of Japan is only about seventy-five miles long, and we pretty much stayed on the base. For most of us, there were only two things to do with our free time: become an alcoholic or become an athlete. I chose sports. I started getting into scuba-diving, and I began taking weight-lifting seriously. My first bodybuilding competition was in Japan, and I realized I liked competing. After leaving Japan, I was stationed back in Illinois for three and a half years, before eventually being transferred to San Diego. My final duty station was at the El Toro Marine Base in Orange County, California, the county I still call home.

During my tenure in the Marines, I learned all about the necessity of being detail-oriented. As a staff sergeant, my experience included training incoming reserves, supervising a crew of maintenance personnel, conducting inspections of F-78 aircraft, as well as RF-4B, KC-130, and UH-1E planes. I was also involved in the quality control of the Corps' multimillion-dollar technical publications.

Being a Marine taught me something my mother had been trying to teach me my whole life. *D-i-s-c-i-p-l-i-n-e*, to learn and accept responsibility for your actions.

When I left the Marine Corps after eleven years, I'd become a world-class bodybuilder. In the thirty-three competitions listed on my bodybuilding profile, in over half of them I took home first prize. In 1985 alone, I won first place in every competition I was in. The titles range from Mr. Grandprix (Japan), Mr. Pacific U.S.A., Mr. Western America, and Mr. Michelangelo Bodybuilding Champ. The last year I competed nationally was 1995, I took second place in the Mr. World Bodybuilding Championships.

By the time I left the service in 1989, I'd already moved in a couple different directions. The Corps gave me a huge, giant stepping-stone to try different things. I started my own vitamin business, worked as a personal trainer and began working as a jailer for the Orange County jail system in 1986, while I was on reserve. I was hesitant about it because I felt like I was leaving one green uniform and going into another. But it was an easy transition to make, so I did it. I had two jobs. I worked the "Gate House"— I checked inmates in, I did bookings. I oversaw people doing their weekend jail time.

For example, if you have a 502, or a DUI, you might have to serve a weekend sentence. The men who would come through would be booked and then walked back to the receiving area. We'd take their clothes and put them into a property storage in exchange for a yellow jumpsuit, and then they'd wear it around for the weekend. Come Sunday, if they didn't get into any trouble, we would return their clothing about five P.M. and send them back outside. I also worked in Receiving, where they'd bus in inmates in their civilian clothes or coming from another jail, and we'd have to get them changed and prepped for our jail.

Some pretty exciting things went on. Some pretty funny things, too. I slammed this Mexican kid into a gate one time. He was talking shit coming into Receiving. He was being transferred to our jail and a lot of people who came through, had something to prove to show they were a badass. He was talking shit in broken Spanish, telling me I dropped my wallet, saying anything to get me to turn around and pay attention to him. I was running Receiving at that time, and I completely turned the whole department around. Before I came, it was mismanaged and after eleven years of Marine Corps detail, I knew a few things about organization. I was in charge when this kid shows up, and he starts up, pulling his shit, and I wasn't gonna put up with it. First off, I couldn't put up with it, because you had to let these characters know who was running the place from the get-go. In addition, he was bothering me.

As I was taking him toward the laundry area to get his inmate clothes, as soon as he passed through this one gate, I slammed him through the gate, and as he hit, he tried to slam it back and then I slammed it again. I caught him going between the gate. Needless to say, inmates have rights, he wrote me up, and I had to go see the watch commander. I told him what happened. They called it a grievance report. Nothing came of it. That was it, and it went away. But word got around that I wasn't a jailer to fuck with.

Some of these guys were just plain crazy, though. I was on duty one morning when an inmate had to register for his weekend jail time. I smelled him coming before I saw him. He was a white guy, about five foot nine, 180 pounds, and he was really greasy, greasier than an auto mechanic who's spent the day under a car. The guy was grimy, and he just stank, real bad. I looked at the other deputy who was on duty that morning, and he looked at me back, and silently we stared at one another, like, "Uh-uh, something's wrong here." The guy just came from work, and he drove like this in his car. It was all wrong.

We began processing him, and at that point, we left him just butt-ass naked, just standing there. We began searching his clothes. The smell was very distinctive but we couldn't find anything. He's standing there, looking like he's thinking, *Oh shit.* We searched and searched but we still couldn't track anything down. I wasn't about to let this muthafucka pull anything on us. Just as we gave him his inmate clothes, both the deputy and I looked at one another again and said, "The shoes!"

Dude almost had us. The shoes were so saturated with grease and oil, he knew we weren't going to want to touch them. He was wrong. We picked them up and threw 'em on the counter. We started pulling them apart from the inside and sure enough, we found PCP. We found the shit under the soles. He'd cut out an area to stash the drugs. He was trying to hide the smell of the PCP with the oil smell, but the combination of the two was putting out an odor that was unfamiliar yet familiar. So we knew something was up.

This dude was planning to do a little side business while he was doing his weekend time. It wasn't unusual for this kind of shit to go down, but in this case, he was the only one going down. We rolled him up, and he got arrested immediately on the spot. He went from being a weekender in a minimum-facility prison to going in front of a judge who hit him up for possession, smuggling, and trying to escape. He's probably still wishing he never met us.

During my time as an O.C. jailer, which lasted about a year and a half, I had the opportunity to work a variety of jobs. I always need excitement because I get bored pretty easily, so I moved around a lot within the system. One of these moves included working "Visiting."

For those of you on the outside, who've never had a family member on lockdown, let me just tell you that Visiting is fuckin' hilarious. In jail, it doesn't get any better than visiting days. The inmate's family and friends would come to the jail and each one had to fill out a visiting slip, explaining who they were. This slip would go to the front desk and a guard would make an announcement, "Inmate So-and-so, you have a visitor." He only made the announcement twice.

The guests would be allowed in the waiting area. We didn't search them but we could if we wanted to. As a courtesy we usually didn't, because it was a minimum-security joint. About nine times out of ten, men and women both were trying to smuggle shit inside. The way it worked is, one of the inmates would go into the visiting area, and there were three deputies, one at each end, walking up and down each aisle, while another was stationed nearby to watch everything that went down.

You gotta be really sharp in Visiting, and I actually liked it. You'd get to see the different people coming in, and, man, you just have to see it to believe it. There were more guests who looked like they should be in prison than prisoners. The people in the Orange County jail system are primarily Latino, with a smaller percentage of whites and blacks. The majority of guests were women, because the inmates are primarily male, and it was funny to watch the scenarios.

We took classes on smuggling, and we knew they would try to play us. Often, they thought they were pulling shit over on us, and a lot of times they did, but usually we saw it coming. You had to be like a hawk staring down looking for your dinner to come by, a rat or a field mouse.

A woman would go to kiss her man, the only thing separating them was a table. There wasn't no glass or no phone. A girl would go to embrace or kiss the inmate, and what you'd have to look for is a blow from the female. If you saw her blowing in his mouth, you know what she was up to. That's the only way to pass a heavy object, meaning a balloon with marijuana in it, or PCP, or cocaine.

Any inmate that we thought had just received any drugs or something orally, we'd pluck him out of there, put him in a special holding cell and wait. There would be nothing in there except for a toilet. We'd feed him, we'd give him everything he needed to drink, and we'd Ex-Lax their ass. Nine times out of ten, we'd catch 'em. The person who came in would be busted, too, because they have to show ID, and since an inmate is only allowed one visitor on any given day, you can rest assured the visitor would get a visit of her own.

There was so much shit going down—and what's a trip is, some of the women were just gorgeous. I'd see a beautiful-looking woman signing up to see an inmate and I'd wonder, *What does she see in him?* The mutha-fucka's in jail, and she's standing behind him, supporting him. Some of the deputies would try to pick up on them, and there was this one particular cat who had it going on with one of the inmates' girls. He bragged to the inmate about it and just fucked with the guy senseless. But the girl denied it, so the prisoner just thought the deputy was messing with him. He wasn't. He was fucking his bitch. What can I say? It takes two to tango.

The deputies and the inmates always fucked with each other, though. It's how they passed the time. In Visiting, when you have to call the name of the inmate, we even used to play pranks on the deputy who was calling the names. We'd make up our own slips, with bullshit names on them. Over the intercom, we'd hear the deputy going: "Attention inmates, attention inmates, Visiting is about to start. Please listen up for your name. . . . "

He'd always go by last name first. Without even thinking, he'd read whatever name was in front of him, so sure enough, over the intercom, you might hear: "Inmate Meoff, inmate Meoff, you have a visitor, inmate Jack Meoff." Everybody would start cracking up, the deputy, the prisoners, the visitors, everybody. They got me, too. The first time it happened, I was in tears. There were so many ways to mess with inmates and deputies at the same time. It was like a game, we had fun. We made the best of a crazy situation.

The way I sum up my jailing experience is, you're an overpaid baby-sitter. That's what a jail is. You get paid a lot of money to watch these guys fuck up. I had some pretty cool inmates, not all of them are bad guys. Some of them would commit crimes out of desperation, they'd have lost their job and in order to try to survive and to keep their families fed, they'd do dirt. Some couldn't afford child support, or were in there for a DUI and couldn't pay a Johnny Cochran to bail them out. If they were cool with me, then I was cool with them. That's just how I am with everybody. It didn't matter what their status was. I didn't look down on them because they were in prison. I don't care about shit like that.

I had a friend who was a nine-year veteran cop, who pulled a 211 not long ago—armed robbery. Now his ass is sitting in jail, same jail I used to work in. This guy was so cool, he'd give you the shirt off his back. He was too generous. He fell behind in his debt, had some financial problems, and got desperate. He hit up a jewelry store, had it all planned out with a partner, but he fucked up. He didn't disguise himself, and they caught him.

He just called me the other day. He knows how I feel about him. I've told him no one can change our friendship, what he did he has to live with, but he's still the same person I knew and hung out with. The only difference is, we're not going to be able to hang out and do the same shit we used to do. He never fucked with me, so why should I stop associating myself with him? It's not like he was a good guy, and now he's a bad guy.

I told him not to feel like he doesn't have any friends, because he does. The sad thing is, he did lose a lot of his friends. The bottom line is, a lot of people don't want to associate with you when you're down on your luck. That's when people are their loneliest and it's also when they're the most vulnerable. It's what makes people commit crimes. I'm not the one who's gonna judge him. He did the crime, now he's doing the time. The only one who can judge him is the Almighty.

It's the same thing with inmates. There are some who are totally cool and some who are dirtbags. You have good inmates who are dirtbags, also. There's a reason they're in jail. Smart people are not sitting in jail, dumb people are in jail. Sometimes smart people do stupid things. If you're sitting behind bars, regardless of what got you there, you did something stupid. When your freedom's taken from you, and your family is taken from you, you're not smart.

The sad thing is, where I came from, most of my friends ended up dead or in prison, and what I learned from working within the system is, there's fairness and unfairness. I saw a lot of unfairness—both inside and outside of the prison system.

When you work for the Orange County Sheriff's Department, you're supposed to be promoted out of the jail system to a patrolling officer at the end of two years, but the only people getting the promotions were people with college degrees. I have a buddy who's been stuck in that job for eight years. He only has a high-school diploma, and he needs the job, he's got a family to support. Guards like my buddy wind up doing more time in the jail system than they originally signed up for. It's fucked-up, but like I said, there's fairness and unfairness. The longer you stay in the jail, the more likely you start to become like the inmates. Hard.

Ultimately, I'd had my taste of law enforcement and decided I didn't want any more part of it.

CHAPTER THREE

KASH, PRINCE OF EARS

Sometimes, when I look back at my life now, I trip out on the way things happened. It seems as if everything, in some way, was leading up to me working with Death Row Records, and specifically Tupac Shakur, the greatest young rapper of our time.

One of the things I know Pac liked about me from the start was the fact I had my game down long before I hooked up with Death Row. He didn't like anybody who seemed to be a starfucker. I wasn't into any of that shit. What I had, I'd earned myself. Death Row didn't give me anything I hadn't already gotten on my own.

By the time I was an adult, I never did anything if there wasn't money involved, so when I started working for Wrightway Security, which was owned by one of Suge's homeboys, Reggie Wright, I already owned a home in Laguna Beach and had nice cars. It impressed Tupac that I'd show up to work driving a Nissan Twin Turbo 300ZX or a Mercedes Benz 500SL convertible. I wasn't looking to get on Death Row's gravy train.

For me, it started out as just another job, just a way to keep the cash flow coming. In fact, I made about $300 a day less working for Wrightway than I made in my first gig as a bodyguard, and believe it or not, the man I worked for was just as notorious as most of Death Row's players.

His name was Kashimar Pashakhan, but he told everyone to just call him Kash. I'd originally met Kash in 1984 at a gym called Superflex; he used to teach Tae Kwon Do and he held the highest-level belt possible. He was into martial arts big-time. We weren't friends but we were buddies, we were cool with one another.

He disappeared for a few years, and I didn't see him again for five years. The next time I saw Kash was at this hole-in-the-wall gym called

South Coast. He came running over to me: "Frank! How the heck you doing?"

We got caught up and he tells me he's been working for a mortgage company. "Check out what I'm driving." He takes me outside and shows me a Corniche Rolls-Royce. I figure the mortgage-banking life's been good to him.

We promised to see each other again, and a few months went by before I ran into Kash at Ken Norton's Gold's Gym. Ken Norton's a boxer who fought Ali, Foreman, and Frazier, and he had bought a Gold's franchise in Lake Forest, California. By now it's October 1989, and I asked him, again, where he's been.

"Ah, Frank I'm on the move," he says. Then he introduces me to his bodyguard, Terry.

I asked him why he needed a bodyguard and he said, "That's right, you don't know." He takes me aside and tells me a lot's gone down since the last time we'd met. He then reveals he's actually an Iranian prince and his family was just recently able to go public with their title. "It was hush-hush, and nobody could know about it," he said. "We were in danger for years, as long as the Shah was alive."

He offered me a job on the spot. Would I like to be his bodyguard?

I'd already gotten disillusioned with law enforcement, I was separated from my wife at the time, the mother of my daughter Vanessa, and I thought, *Why not?*

Kash told me the pay was $500 a day, and we'd be traveling a lot because he liked to gamble. I started working that same weekend.

They told me to go to the John Wayne Airport in O.C., where there'd be a ticket waiting for me to fly to Las Vegas. "All my guys wear black," he said. "I need you to do that for me."

Dressed in black from head to toe, I went to the airport and the ticket was waiting for me. Kash was staying at Caesar's Palace, and I met him at the baccarat table. He was a serious high roller. I watched him gamble away $70,000 in a hand. When he was winning or on a roll, he'd hand me chips. By the time the night was over, he'd given me $3,000 worth of chips and all I'd done was sit with him at the table while he gambled. He told me I'd brought him good luck and said he wanted me standing to his right whenever he gambled.

For as long as he was gambling, we never sat down, he always wanted us on our feet. We never quit gambling until his wife, Jody, was ready to go to bed. That's usually when the real partying began and Kash would hit the nightclubs. He was a ladies' man, and a drinker, and it was our job to accompany him, whenever, wherever, and whatever the situation. It didn't take me long to learn Kash didn't want any of his guards near the women, who always managed to snake their way around the high rollers.

Not one time did any of us fuck around with women on the job. We never picked up on any ladies, because Kash wouldn't allow it. There were no questions asked. During the day, we'd be "buddy, buddy, buddy," working out, breaking bread together, doing everything together. At night, while on the job, we didn't dare even catch the eye of a woman. Our only objective was to protect his ass.

I worked with Kash for a few weeks before he decided he wanted more bodyguards. I suggested to him I put together a security team who could travel each weekend from California to Vegas. He liked the idea and told me, "I want all brothas. I want the biggest, blackest muthafuckas you can find."

I told him, "No problem." I hit up a couple of my friends, he interviewed them, and it was cool. I ended up putting together a team of about six guards, which meant he traveled with an entourage of nine guys total.

Everyone saw Kash coming, he made sure of that. He wanted to be surrounded by bodyguards because it made him look good. He was rollin' with so much money, he didn't care what it was costing him.

When you're getting paid that kind of money, you don't ask questions. I became his 24-7 man. He trusted me with every single thing he did. Ultimately, I took care of all his personal business. I had keys to his car, I handled his family affairs, and became the guy people spoke to when they wanted to get to Kash.

Just like with Tupac, who eventually singled me out from the other security guards, it became clear to Kash I was the most responsible person out of his bodyguard crew. Pac understood this quality about me—that when it came down to business, I handled his business.

Playtime came after work, when everything was over, but business was business.

Kash only played craps and baccarat, and the Las Vegas police had their eye on him. They'd even given him a name. They called him "the Prince of Darkness," because he'd only come out at night and when he did, he was surrounded by big black men dressed all in black. He was only twenty-seven or twenty-eight years old at the time. He was spending so much money, it was sick. Whenever we went anywhere, it was always first-class. He leased out private planes to fly to Vegas and Reno, and once we were there, we'd have entire hotel floors to ourselves. I remember one New Year's Eve, he took over one hundred rooms at the Mirage in Vegas. Kash didn't fuck around. Nobody paid for anything. Kash took care of all of us, and everything else was comped.

A year later, I would learn the true source of Kash's income.

He had women around him all the time. He'd ask them to join his table, and they'd flock to him. We'd party at this club called the Shark Club, and if somebody stared at him or looked at his wife or his girlfriend—it didn't matter who it was—he would freak out. He'd flip, he'd just lose his fucking mind. He'd tell one of his bodyguards, "Bring him here!" Someone would go over and tell the guy, "The Prince wants to see you." They'd bring the guy over and Kash would get in his face, yelling, "Why are you looking at me?!" Kash was real paranoid.

One time at the Shark Club, a photographer was taking pictures while Kash was on the dance floor, and we didn't know who the guy was. We were scattered throughout the club, and all of a sudden, the photographer takes off running. So we took off after him. Turns out there were two of them. We caught the guy with the camera, took the camera and took the film, but the other guy got out onto the Strip. Kash was furious because he liked to fight, and he wanted the guy for himself.

I can't count the number of times he'd get into a fight behind a club. He'd either force his victim to fight or he'd just kick the shit out of him. He seemed to beat people up for fun. Then it got to the point where it was serious.

He liked to fight, he knew how to fight, and he took home his trophy. Most of the time, it wasn't even a match. Kash was deadly. He was seriously into martial arts and knew what he was doing.

We were in Lake Tahoe when some serious shit went down. The guards on that day included me and some guys from my team, Kenny, Greg, and Raoul. Kash took us skiing, and we were gambling. His wife was with us on that trip and there was a guy on the other side of our table, behind the dealer, and he was staring at Kash and his wife. Kash was a real nervous person, he started sweating, and he was rolling, and as usual, we were all dressed in our black-suit uniforms. We wore black shades at all times so nobody could see our eyes.

There's two guys on each side of Kash, and two in the crowd, and this young dude, he's about twenty-six years old, keeps staring at us and laughing, and he's clearly drunk. Kash is getting really angry. "That muthafucka keeps staring at me and Jody, and it's pissing me off," he said.

What was really going down was the guy was trying to fuck with us, not Kash. He was just drunk and fucking around, and he wanted to mess with us. We were staring back stone-faced. He couldn't crack a smile from any of us. We're looking at him, like, *You fuckin' idiot, get away.* I'm muttering under my breath, "Just go. Get the fuck away." I wanted to save the guy some trouble. But he wouldn't back off. He continued from a distance, antagonizing us, and antagonizing Kash. So our Prince says, "Go get him."

I watched the guy walk to the bathroom, and me and Kenny followed him. The other two flanked Kash. While the guy goes to take a piss at the urinal, Kenny goes to his right and I go to his left. He's smack in the middle. Kenny says to him, "Why the fuck you laughing, punk?"

The guy says, "What the fuck are you talking about?"

Kenny goes to guard the door and the dude is shaking his dick by this time. I grab him by the back of his head and slam him into the front of the wall of the urinal. He bounces off it and starts running toward the door, but Kenny's there to catch him. We whoop the guy's ass. We go back out and tell Kash it's been handled but he needs to see some blood. So we show him a handkerchief caked with blood. We each got a $500 bonus that night.

We didn't kick the guy's ass because of the bonus, we would have handled the situation regardless. It was part of our job. If the guy hadn't been an asshole, there wouldn't have been a problem.

As the night wore on, Kash continued to gamble. There was no place to party in Tahoe, so when he was through gambling, we all went back to the hotel. It was already the next day and Kash decided he wanted to go skiing. Everyone was scheduled to meet Kash in the lobby of his lodge, but before he could get downstairs, we get a phone call.

"Is this Mr. Pashakhan's room?"

I answered, "Yes, it is."

"May I please speak with him?"

"No," I said. "He's unavailable at the moment."

"Is this his assistant?"

I said, "Yes."

The person on the other end explained it was the front desk and it was urgent.

Kash grabbed the phone and said, "Who the fuck is this?"

They put him through to the hotel manager, who explained we needed to leave the hotel within a half an hour.

Kash leaped up and lunged toward the door; while I grabbed him, Terry grabbed the phone and asked what the fuck was going on.

"Sir, two of Mr. Pashakhan's bodyguards beat up a son of a United States senator last night, and if you aren't out of here in a half an hour, the entourage will be under arrest."

The manager explained the son was a drunk and apologized for any inconvenience, but nevertheless offered to escort us out of the state.

We all scrambled around and got everything packed within five minutes. The only problem was, we were snowed in. The hotel had to round up a bunch of 4-Runners to drive us out of the state's limits. Wherever Kash stayed, everything was comped. He was a high roller, so all of our rooms, our food, our transportation, was free. They needed us out of there, and they couldn't put us on a plane, so they had to physically drive us out of Tahoe and into Reno. We had flown in on a private plane and obviously we weren't going out on one because of the weather conditions.

Reno didn't have any snow, but we stayed through Sunday anyway, and there were no more incidents. Needless to say, we never went back to Tahoe. Kash didn't like Tahoe anymore.

He did, however, still go to Las Vegas, and we continued to fly there nearly every weekend. One of his favorite clubs to party at was a club called Botney's. I didn't learn until way later that Botney's became 662, Suge Knight's club in Vegas. I didn't learn about this until the day Tupac got shot. We were in a security meeting preparing for the post-fight-night party, and an attorney told us about the club's history. It knocked me on my feet. I used to party there with Kash in '89. He liked the club because it was owned by this Persian cat, and they treated him like royalty. It was a really elegant club and, even back then, it was a hip-hop club.

As fate would have it, I was scheduled to work there again, only this time, it was 662, Suge Knight's club, and I was bodyguarding for Death Row.

I thought I was gonna work for Kash for a long time. We clicked, and he took good care of me. In return, I took good care of him. When October of 1990 rolled around, however, Kash's high-rollin' days came to an abrupt end. Turns out G-Money over here was accused of embezzling from mortgage companies.

The police claimed that Kash's cash game was to get loans approved by mortgage companies for phony people or for people who've died. I was handling his personal affairs and I'd see these checks coming in for $900,000 and didn't think twice. He not only boasted about family money, but as far as I knew, he was a legitimate mortgage broker—a high roller all around. I used to carry cash for him and sometimes had as much as a quarter million on me. Kash liked me for a lot of reasons, but one reason in particular was trust. He knew he could rely on me to be honest with his affairs.

He ended up getting busted and he fled the country. I never saw him or heard from him again.

When I started bodyguarding for Death Row, I thought of him once or twice, half expecting to see him at a craps table, talking loudly and surrounded by his all-black entourage.

I never did, though. Instead, I was the one surrounded by an all-black entourage, a crew comprised of Tupac Shakur and his young soldiers, the Immortal Outlaws, and usually about a dozen Compton Bloods, all working for the man Las Vegas police believed to be the New Prince of Darkness, Marion "Suge" Knight.

PART TWO

DEATH ROW

CHAPTER FOUR

WRIGHTWAY SECURITY

No one from Death Row talks, so most of the reports you read are filled with speculation and secondhand information, sometimes accurate, sometimes not, but never telling the full story. Occasionally, Suge Knight himself will step up and answer some questions from the media. Suge, however, isn't going to tell you what's really going down because there's nothing in it for him.

On certain levels, Suge's a very intelligent businessman, and to be honest, I enjoyed working for him. Before he was known as the chief executive officer of Death Row Records—the record company he founded with attorney David Kenner and the company that changed rap music forever by releasing Dr. Dre's *The Chronic* and Snoop Doggy Dogg's *Doggystyle* albums within a year—he had been a bodyguard for N.W.A., the original gangsta-rap supergroup from Compton, which launched the careers of Dr. Dre, Ice Cube, and Eazy-E, all formidable rap talents.

Suge appreciated the value of a bodyguard, and treated security with respect. To get the job working for Wrightway, it didn't take a certain individual. There were no height, or size, or muscular specifications coming from Death Row.

It took a badge. Although Reggie Wright owned the company, Suge had set him up and called all the shots. His first specification was all members of security had to be retired or off-duty policemen, period. Even Reggie had been a Compton police officer before he began working for Suge.

Suge wanted the guards to be able to keep them out of trouble and to neutralize situations. It was always instilled in us that we were there to be credible witnesses when they fucked up. That was the main reason they needed off-duty police officers. They weren't looking for the average person who's just walking around with credentials. It wasn't an issue of how big I was, although that became a plus for me. Later, when I worked with Tupac, I know it was a factor. He'd nicknamed me "Big Frank," and I think he liked having a big-ass nigga on his side.

In fact, Suge, at six foot three inches tall and 330 pounds, must have appreciated my size, and the work it took to get there. He lifted weights also and he knew people were intimidated by his size. I was the biggest employee around the Death Row camp, and I fit right in to what they wanted in a bodyguard.

I began working for Death Row in September 1995, the same month Tupac was released on $1.5 million bail, after serving eight months at Riker's Island in upstate New York for sexual assault. Suge had posted the bail, and in return Tupac was to record three albums for Death Row.

I don't know if you believe in fate, but I got the job through what can only be described as destiny.

One of my buddies, K. J., worked for a limousine service that Death Row used. One day, he'd picked up Tupac to bring him to the Death Row recording studio, Can-Am, which was located out in Tarzana, California, in the San Fernando Valley area. While he was killing time waiting for Tupac to finish recording, he struck up a conversation with another friend of mine, Cedric, who was working security for Wrightway. Cedric and I spent almost a decade together in the Marines, and I hadn't talked to him since I'd left the service. Cedric, Suge, and Reggie Wright had all grown up in the same Compton neighborhood. K. J. and Cedric somehow got on the subject of bodybuilding, and my name came up. Cedric couldn't believe K. J. knew me, and he asked him for my phone number.

That night, I got a ring from Cedric, who thought I was still working in the Sheriff's Department, and we caught up with each other. I told him all about Kash and my bodyguarding days, and he tripped out, because Wrightway had just put out the word they were looking for another guard. At the time, I was looking for work, and Cedric encouraged me to send my résumé to Wrightway Security.

I figured, *Why not?* I knew all about Death Row's reputation, but figured they couldn't be up to anything worse than the shit that went down in my old neighborhood, so I got a résumé together and enclosed one of my bodybuilding portraits. I gave it to Cedric, who gave it to Reggie. Little did I know, by then Larry Condiff was out of the joint and working as Wrightway Security's office manager, Reggie's right-hand man.

"Before I even saw the résumé," recalls Larry, "I heard Cedric talking about a potential new security guard and when he said his name was Frank Alexander, my head snapped around—'Frank Alexander?!' I knew he was out here somewhere but didn't know where, and I figured it couldn't be my homeboy Frank. It would be too coincidental."

Cedric showed Larry the picture. "I looked at it and said, 'I'll be damned,' " says Larry.

He called me right away, and it was like a blast from the past. We both couldn't believe it. Immediately, we started talking about the old neighborhood. Larry told me he'd been back three times since I left and each time, he wished he had a faster ticket home. We talked about some of the old Manor homies, most of 'em dead. His best friend was Johnny Brown's younger brother, Alan, who also ended up dead. Both of us still have all our family back there, and even though they all hate Chicago, they're afraid to pull up roots. Besides, some of them are in pretty deep. My family's tight with the Folks (the G.D.'s), the gang that runs Chicago today.

It was cool catching up and I was happy to hear Larry was doing good, married with a couple of kids. He said he liked working for Wrightway, and he hooked me up with an interview with Reggie, but he warned me, straight up, "Reggie's a punk, keep an eye on your paycheck and everything will be cool." Cedric said the same thing. Every payday, some drama would go down, but I figured I'd be straight up with the guy, let him know I'm no punk.

I drove to the city of Paramount, where Wrightway is located, the next day. Paramount's an unremarkable, industrial area in South Los Angeles, about a half an hour away from Can-Am studios. Reggie was about two or three hours late, and Larry told me that's pretty much what I could expect from him. By the time he showed up, I was already on my way back to Orange County. He paged me and said he was ready to meet with me so I turned around.

Reggie Wright's about five foot seven and somewhere around 260 pounds. From what I could tell, his most impressive characteristic was being friends with Suge Knight. Technically, he was Suge's bodyguard and they were tight as brothers.

I was very direct with him. I let him know I'm a loyal muthafucka, and I've never bitten the hand that feeds me. I wanted him to understand I wasn't gonna take any shit from him, but in return, he'd get one dependable employee. I learned later, he was the kind of guy who didn't trust anyone, because he couldn't trust himself.

I got the job and began working in the studio the next day. The Can-Am recording studio is located on Oxnard Avenue in Tarzana. It was Death Row's main place of business before they bought their own $5 million building on Wilshire Boulevard, in a posh business district of Los Angeles. But the whole time I worked with them, they recorded at Can-Am. Tarzana is the last place anybody would expect to find Death Row's players. It's a quiet, low-key part of the San Fernando Valley, surrounded by nothing but working class white people and Mexicans. I think Suge probably liked the anonymity Can-Am afforded him. Unless you knew what was going on, you'd never find out where they were.

Even if you did, there were two security guards on duty at all times, one stationed in the lobby, with a metal detector to wand people on their way into the recording areas. The other was in the control room, manning the security cameras, which showed everything taking place throughout the entire facility. Everyone entered through the lobby, and everyone got wanded before being allowed entry. Everybody except the artists, that is.

Suge's office was inside Can-Am, and it was huge. He had it done up to suit him, with a big old Death Row logo in the middle of the carpet in the floor, and of course, the whole office was bloodred. Suge Knight displayed his gang affiliation to the Compton-based Bloods the way a doctor hangs his M.D. certificate for clients to view. It was sort of Suge's own certificate of authenticity. Some people are members of the Elk's Lodge, and some people are gangstas. Suge was a gangsta. He's the one who created the rules we abided by, and no matter who you were or who you were with, you got checked upon entrance.

The first time I ever met Pac was in the studio, not long after his release from Riker's Island, the New York prison where he'd spent the previous eight months of his life. Whenever he showed up, he was usually tailed by the Immortal Outlaws, five of the coolest guys you'd want to meet. They were all in their teens, except Malcolm, he was twenty-one, and they were all part of Pac's posse. There was Muta, Malcolm, Yak, Fatal, and Kay. Each of them had the nicknames Pac had given them tattooed on the left side of their necks, including Pac, who went by Makaveli. Malcolm was Edi, Yak was Kadafi, Fatal was Whosane aka Hussein—all gangsta leaders hated by Americans.

I didn't pay much attention to Pac at first. We passed each other in the studio with little more than a nod or an occasional handshake. I was a generation older than most of these guys and had little interest in the music before I began working with Death Row. I only knew Tupac on his reputation, and what I knew, I didn't necessarily like.

I liked the job, though. It was entertaining. Something was always there to amuse you. In the time I worked lobby security, I found Glocks, 9-millimeters, big-ass Bowie knives. I'd just politely ask whoever owned the weapon to return it to the car. They didn't like that one bit, because they felt safer being strapped. Nevertheless, rules were rules and we had to abide by them. Weed didn't follow under security jurisdiction. Bags and bags of pot flowed into Can-Am, like there was an endless train unloading it at the doorstep. The studio was interesting because it's where everyone got a chance to get familiar with each other. The artists got to check out security, and alternately, we got to check out the artists. Everyone's first reaction to me was to just trip on my size. I was the biggest member of the security team and I used to get a lot of recognition for it. Suge had even installed a gym in the studio, he took weight-lifting pretty seriously.

The other members of Wrightway's team, like myself, came from backgrounds that included law enforcement. Aside from Cedric, who originally introduced me to Wrightway and was my friend from the Corps, there was Kevin Hackie, a Compton police officer who had worked with Reggie Wright on the force going back ten years. Reggie's father, Reggie Wright, Sr., was still a high-ranking lieutenant in Compton, and Kevin also knew him. The Outlaws nicknamed Kevin "Robocop," because he had a militant style and knew the law like the back of his hand.

Another Inglewood reserve police officer, Leslie Gaulden, came to Wrightway with nine years of executive protection under his belt. There was Cooper, who worked for San Bernardino's police department, along with Al Gittens, who eventually became a Wrightway supervisor. There was also Marcus and Kenneth, both of whom were reserve officers for the

Inglewood force. The only member without a police background was Michael Moore, who worked as fire captain for Moreno Valley, a suburb outside of L.A. County.

People have this idea that Death Row employees were all just a bunch of thugs and gangstas looking to do dirt. The reality was, most of the employees I met were hardworking, intelligent people who showed an extreme loyalty to Suge. Many of them had never had a job in their lives before Suge offered them one. Wrightway employees were no different. They were first-rate guys, and the only difference between them and Death Row's employees, was they held a badge.

CHAPTER FIVE

SNOOP AND THA DOGG POUND

Reggie approached me one day in the studio and told me he needed me to go to New York for four days in December. "You're gonna be bodyguarding Snoop, Kurupt, and Nate Dogg," he said.

I thought, *Cool.* It was my first trip with Death Row, and I figured it might be interesting.

It was interesting, alright. Tha Dogg Pound was a trip, young rappers with a lot of attitude, all led by Snoop Doggy Dogg, one of the coolest muthafuckas on this planet. Snoop's as laid-back as his music, and I liked being around him. Daz was a young producer, who was being groomed to take over a lot of Death Row's production duties. Nate Dogg and Kurupt are the rappers who make up Tha Dogg Pound, and while I didn't know too much about Nate, aside from the fact he was an ex-Marine—but he didn't talk about that too much—I'd already heard all the Kurupt stories. Let's put it this way, his name suited him.

Kurupt was already having serious problems. He was too young to be living so fast, and by the time I came to Death Row, it seemed no one was really looking out for him. Kurupt was originally from Philly, and he was introduced to Death Row by his former managers, two guys named the Brumfeld Brothers. He got a recording deal, but Suge gangsta'd him away from his managers and appointed his wife, Sharetha, as manager. Sharetha also managed Snoop.

Kurupt didn't waste any time getting into trouble when he came to Death Row. When I got there, Reggie had him bouncing from one security guard to the next and no one wanted to deal with him.

I figured he was just young and he hadn't learned how to handle his business yet. I remember him paging me one time when I was off duty and at home with my wife. He'd gotten into a huge fight with Al Gittens, because apparently he brought so much weed into the studio Al had to step in and ask him to remove it. It wasn't a baggie, but more like a grocery bag. Kurupt refused and a fight ensued. His basic problem is when he drinks, he gets *drunk*. When he gets high, he gets *high*. His little body couldn't handle the combination. Kurupt looked like he weighed 100 pounds dripping wet, and he was trying to keep up with the big boys.

Marcus was assigned to Snoop, and this was when Snoop was still on lockdown from the shooting of Philip Woldemariam, an L.A. resident who'd threatened Snoop a few times. The guy showed up at a park and started menacing Snoop and his crew, and his bodyguard at the time—who I found out later I knew from bodybuilding—saw the guy reach for a gun, and before he could pull it out, the bodyguard shot and killed him. Snoop was allowed to go to New York because we were there to shoot a video for the "New York, New York" single, off Tha Dogg Pound's first CD, *Dogg Food*, and the judge must've seen the logic in us having to film it on location.

Everyone was hedging about working with Kurupt, so I ended up with him primarily. Leslie, who was looking after Nate on that trip, had already experienced Mr. Kurupt, as he called him, and warned me about him. "When I first started working with him, I hated his guts. Everyone did," recalls Leslie. "I told Frank he could have him. Frank for some reason, seemed to be so patient with Kurupt, and started to mold him. Later on, I could see some shifts in his personality. At first, though, he wanted to be a gangsta so bad."

Les is right, and I used to tell him rappers are not gangstas. What gangstas do you know—Scarface, John Gotti—go running around dropping names on everybody? Rappers drop everybody's fuckin' name that they can on a record. Gangstas don't talk. They're quiet. There's a code of silence. "But Kurupt was typical of a lot of young kids," says Leslie. "They ain't never had anything in their lives, but they have a talent and a knack for this rap game. They start making a little bit of money and with this young mind and hood-rat mentality, they think their shit don't stink."

The first day Leslie worked with Kurupt, he put his badge in his face, and said, "You ain't gonna like what I've got to say, but I'll tell you what this means—this means, when you're with me, you will abide by the fuckin' law, period."

Like most of Death Row's artists, a little discipline went a long way.

Later on, before Kurupt left for the "Freaknik" in Atlanta, the black version of Spring Break, he thanked Les for watching out for his ass.

After what went down in New York, I became his bona fide superhero.

New York

We flew in on a Friday and stayed in a Ramada Inn in New Jersey, across the Hudson River. A Ramada Inn in Jersey sounds pretty low-rent for Death Row, but there was a reason they put us up there. Suge didn't want the artists getting in trouble, and the hotel was about thirty miles away from Manhattan. It was a fortune by cab, limos were limited, and it was snowing. Suge wanted to keep their asses out of trouble and make it as difficult as possible for them to be near the action. He did this a lot when we traveled. Even on video shoots, they would put us as far out as they could. Of course, their biggest concern was Kurupt. With his history of starting shit and the combination of all of them together, you never knew what could happen.

I met up with Snoop the next morning, it was the first time we'd met one-on-one outside of the studio. About five of us were walking to his room and before we even got there, you could smell the pot. It was coming up from under the door. Down the road I discovered when they traveled, they usually took every towel they could get their hands on and wedged them under the cracks of the doors. Snoop's dad, Vernon, was in there observing the fun and so was his Uncle Reo, and everybody was real cool.

We spent the day in Times Square, getting material for the video, and at night, Snoop was supposed to be the featured guest of a popular New York radio station. Before we were due to arrive, Biggie Smalls called the station. Notorious B.I.G. was a rapper who used to be friends with Tupac. They had had a big falling-out and there was a lot of bad blood between the Death Row camp and Biggie's label, Bad Boy, which was run by the producer-rapper Sean "Puffy" Combs. If you're a rap fan, you probably know more about it than I do. All I know is, until New York, I didn't even know if the shit was real or not, and I didn't particularly care.

I was about to take interest.

With our own ears, me, Daz, and Nate Dogg heard what Biggie had to say. We were standing by the lowriders we were using for the video, which were parked on a side street in Times Square, ready to go on to the next scene.

Biggie tells the deejay, "I cannot believe New York is allowing Snoop, Tupac, and Tha Dogg Pound to shoot a video in Times Square. What kind of shit is this?" Biggie started dissing the fact the city was allowing Death Row artists on its turf. He thought Tupac was also with us, and that was his big beef, but he was sending out through the radio waves this kind of message. "This is our city, and you know the beef we have with these muthafuckas," he said.

This is when I knew for the first time that this shit was real, this East and West Coast shit. Needless to say, security had a meeting, reminding all of us to stay really tight, and to keep our eyes open and watch what was going on around us. We didn't stop production but we were all on guard.

The rappers started talking about Biggie's call, and everyone was trippin'.

I went over to where Snoop was, and he put his arm around me and starts screaming, "What up, Biggie muthafucka. We here, we here, we got our boys!!! Security's hot, too. C'mon, bitch!!! Bring it on!!! Bring it on!!!"

I'm looking up at this tall, crazy nigga, thinking, *You've got to be muthafuckin' crazy.*"

His whole crew's there and even if you watch the video, they're all throwing up Dogg Pound signs, braggin' about the fact they're from California.

Up and down the streets, all you could see were barricades and police, who were keeping people off the streets and away from our trailers. It was close to wrap time for the night, and it was somewhere around one A.M. We were only three blocks away from the radio station Snoop was supposed to appear at, and we escorted him there.

We got to the station and found the building pitch-black, with no one there to greet us. This interview had been set up before we even left for New York, so we wondered what was up. A security guard came down, and we told him who we were. He called upstairs to the deejay, and the deejay tells the guard—and I quote—"It hasn't been cleared." He said the station manager "forgot" to clear it. Mind you, Snoop Dogg—one of the greatest rappers ever—is in the building, and this punk-ass deejay refused to let us in.

After some more hemming and hawing, he went ahead and told security to allow Snoop upstairs so he could talk to him. Snoop said, "Fuck this, I'm leaving." I told him just to chill for a second in the limo and let us go upstairs and find out what the fuck is going on. The deejay told us the same thing. It hadn't been cleared, *blah, blah, blah,* and all this other bullshit. We left Snoop downstairs, and when we went back to meet up with him. Snoop said, "Let's just get the fuck back to the hotel, it's their loss."

Everything was supposed to have been set up for Snoop's arrival through the studio manager, and I think they just got cold feet, figuring if they let him on the air, someone might come after them. If it had been Pac it would've been a whole 'notha story, but Snoop's a real cool, chill kind of person, and we just went back to the Ramada Inn and played some video games. He loved playing basketball in his room on his Playstation.

We told him we'd be downstairs if they needed us. Sure enough, the groupies always crawl out of the woodwork. Some girls came up to us in the lobby, asking if we were Snoop's bodyguards and we told them we were.

I went back up to Snoop's room and knocked on the door.

"You coming to get some of this," Snoop said, thinking I wanted to play video games.

I told him what was up with the girls. He asked what they looked like, and I told him they were white girls.

He said, "Nah, I don't fuck with white girls." He said I should track down his Uncle Reo, because he might be interested.

I told him, "He's already down there," and everybody in the room started cracking up. I guess Reo's reputation preceded him. Reo's one cool muthafucka, and everyone got a good laugh out of it.

I don't know if Uncle Reo got any sleep but I know I did. We had to get up at six in the morning because seven A.M. was our call time.

We make it to the location, which was in Brooklyn. The next scene was set up around Snoop, Daz, and Kurupt, who were supposed to be coming out of a Brooklyn brownstone, rapping. Despite how cold it was, the snow had melted already, and the producers had to order some fake snow. The trailers were parked about a block away from where the filming was taking place, and all day long, we had to walk back and forth between the set and the trailers.

The security team had a van, and it was parked on a sidewalk to the right of the artists' trailer, which was parked on the street. Keep in mind, it was cold as fuck and it started raining that slushy East Coast rain, so we were wet, too. Every time the director wanted one of the artists, we had to jump out of the van, go to the trailer and walk to the set. If it was time for your artist to go, you had to jump out and move.

Leslie wasn't playing. He was sitting it out in the van, trying to get warm. He had his socks off, his shoes off, his gloves, his jacket, trying to defrost.

I'm looking at him like he's crazy. "How you gonna jump out this van and walk Nate Dogg over to the set?"

"My shoes got a hole in them," he said. He showed me his boots and sure enough, there was a big hole in the sole of one of them. He made out, though. He went down to wardrobe and they found a big pair of Doc Martens in his size. Les got a brand new pair of boots out of the deal.

Somewhere around one-thirty P.M., the director walked over and said he needed Snoop on the set. I go to the van and knocked on the door, telling Snoop he's needed on the set. Snoop was getting his hair braided, and when I opened up the door, there was a backdraft of smoke. Air came in and *whomp*, the smoke just hit me right in the face.

It was the stinkiest bud you ever wanted to smell. This was Dogg Pound bud, I'd never smelled weed like that.

Everybody inside the van started yelling at me, "Close the door, close the door!"

They didn't want any of the smoke to escape, because they wanted to keep inhaling it. So I stepped out and closed the door behind me. The director was persistent, telling me he really needed Snoop out of there, *now*. I told him I already let Snoop know, and we were all still standing out there when Nate Dogg appeared from around the corner with Kenneth.

I walk up the stairs again, and as soon as I open the door, I hear, *Bang! Bang! Bang!*

Fuck, it's gunshots.

They came from across the street, right in front of a corner storefront. Snoop's dad was in the store, as well as a couple of the production people.

There were probably about ten members of the NYPD, as well as members of the Nation of Islam, but they were all down by the set.

The person who fired the shots was in the store before he began shooting and Snoop's dad saw him. Vernon was in there trying to get the store's owner to turn down the Latino music that was blasting, we were parked about twenty-five feet away and we could barely hear anything it was so loud. The dude had been at the store, waiting for Snoop to come out of the trailer, and, fortunately, he got impatient and just started shooting up the trailer.

Before I learned any of this, all I heard were the shots, and I reacted. Without a vest on, I lunged into the trailer with my gun in hand, yelling, "Where's Snoop?" I was trying to find him but it was hard to make out where he was. There were probably about ten people in the trailer total, they're all on the floor, so I started pulling everybody out, one at a time. Security began mobilizing, but nothing was happening with the NYPD. The gunshots were loud, you'd have to be deaf not to hear them, but they never came over to see what was going on.

As I was pulling each one of them out, I remembered that every one of them was fucked-up. I'm just grabbing heads, I start raising heads to see who I've got. I found Daz, and I pulled him out of there and put him on the curb, under the trailer. I pulled Kurupt out of the trailer and threw him onto the curb. I saw one of Snoop's little cousins, and when I finally got to the bottom, I saw Snoop. They'd all dogg-piled on top of him.

"You okay, you okay?" I asked.

"Yeah, I'm alright," he said.

At this point, I've got everybody on the curb, by the side of the trailer. I started throwing them into the security van, one by one. I do a quick head count and look for our driver. He was this cool Puerto Rican guy, but he's nowhere around and he's got the keys. He was down on the set, but when he heard the gunfire, he took off running.

He made it over to us, and we decided to gun the van out of there. He started driving the van in the direction it was pointed in, and I'm screaming, "No, no, no, no!"

The artists were all down on the floor of the van, and Kenneth and I were outside of the van, backing the van up toward the shoot. People were trying to stop us because the street was blocked off for the shoot, and it was a residential, one-way street. The police and the director were telling us to go back the way we came, and I ignored everybody and kept motioning our driver to back up the van. I wasn't about to send these boys in the direction the shooter took off in, it'd be like walking into a fire. Someone could have been waiting for us further down the street.

I kept the van moving down the sidewalk, despite their protests, then I signaled to Kenneth to get back in the van. I hopped in, and we sped off. As soon as we pulled out of Brooklyn and were on our way back to Jersey, everybody started lifting their heads up.

Nate Dogg was the first to start talking. "I thought that nigga was the shooter," he said, pointing to me. "I looked up and all I saw was a gun, and the muthafucka's saying, 'Where's Snoop at?' "

Everybody started making jokes now, patting me on the back and calling me a hero.

It was so insane. You got to remember, they were all fucked-up. When I pulled Kurupt out of the trailer, he was still holding a 40-ouncer in his hand. He was clinging to it, and I remember snatching the bottle out of his hand and throwing it down before tossing him into the van.

We all rendezvoused back to the Ramada Inn, and by the time we got back there, the laughing had stopped. There were death threats at the front desk. People knew we were staying at the hotel, and about three death threats were phoned in directly to Snoop.

We called up Reggie, and he said Suge was going to get the artists out of there. He sent a Lear jet to some private airstrip, I don't know where the hell it was, and I watched Snoop, Daz, and Kurupt all board the plane. It was raining and snowing when they took off, and I prayed they would make it, because I couldn't help but think about the Buddy Holly situation.

That was some drama. We all got left behind, staying for another day. They stopped production immediately and finished it back in L.A. So much for my first experience traveling with Death Row.

We were all trippin', thankful that no one got shot and replaying everything in our heads. After it all was said and done, we started joking about what everybody was doing. Marcus, who's Snoop's bodyguard now along with Kenneth, ran to the front of the trailer after the shots with an umbrella in his hand. We were all laughing about how this nigga wasn't worried about getting shot, just getting wet.

Leslie was behind me doing God knows what, he was only half dressed and wasn't any part of what was going on. Kenneth and I were the only ones handling the business.

That night, I started thinking about the phone call Biggie had made and realized how fucked-up it was. Biggie put it in somebody's head that we had no business there and this person tried to shoot our trailer up and obviously tried to kill someone.

How no one got injured could only be tracked to God's will. There were so many people in the trailer and yet the bullets didn't hit any of them. Someone did score, though, because Snoop had a backpack full of weed that came up missing. He also had a baby pitbull in there, and the pit also turned up missing. Their lives were intact, however.

When I called home to talk to my wife Lori about it, it was already all over the news. We'd only been married for about a year and she was freaking out. When I look back now, I realize this was her first experience with me traveling for Death Row, too, and it must have been hard on her.

By the time, we got home, MTV was doing stories on it. Every paper had an article about the shooting, and Reggie called me, to find out exactly what happened.

"Suge wants to see you," he said.

This was the first time I met with Suge behind closed doors. I was working in the studio on the day we were supposed to meet, and he called me into his office. He also asked me what happened, and I told him everything.

"You know those niggas love you," he said. "I've had three requests for you to be a personal bodyguard. I wish I had everybody who was like you."

I was flattered, because the way I looked at it, I was only doing my job.

"You saved those niggas' lives out there," he said. "The ultimate decision is going to be yours, but Tha Dogg Pound and Snoop don't want to go anywhere with you."

Sure enough, Kurupt was paging me off the hook during this time. He was afraid to leave the house without me by his side. Their album had just hit and everytime they went somewhere, I was assigned to them.

We went to Hawaii to do *The Grind* on MTV. We stayed at this 10-star resort in Honolulu that was so cool. Everytime they did any interviews,

I was with them. I took them to the Soul Train Awards, and whenever Snoop had court appearances, I escorted him there along with Marcus and Kenneth. Tha Dogg Pound usually traveled with Snoop, so we were all working together.

I continued to do my job, and I didn't trip. Even after the incident, I just looked at the experience, like, *Oh well, it's part of my job description.* I moved on because I'm not the type of person to dwell on something. I believe in just moving forward.

Maybe it was the combination of my attitude and professionalism that started the buzz around Death Row, but ever since New York, people looked at me differently. The artists began calling me "Big Frank," and everybody started giving me props. Whenever I was in the studio, I noticed everybody was just loving me, telling me they heard what happened and congratulating me for a good job.

What I didn't know is Tupac had also gotten the word.

One day I got a call from Reggie asking me to accompany Snoop to a court appearance. Marcus and Kenneth were Inglewood reserve policemen and both had a reserve meeting. It was Snoop's most important court date, and I met him at Daz's house at nine A.M. Another rapper was there named Mr. Malik, and apparently, he'd heard the story, too, and hit me up as soon as I got there.

"I heard about you man, you're Big Frank, right?" he said.

I nodded.

"I want to get at you a little later, I need your digits," he said. "I may need you to roll with me a few times, what's it gonna cost me?"

I told him I worked for Death Row, but if he needed me when I was off duty, it would cost him about $500 a day.

He said, "That's cool. I'll talk to my record company, and maybe we can work something out."

The truth is, most bodyguards at that level make $500 a day, that's what I made working for Kash. We were getting robbed by Reggie, and I knew it.

We continued to roll and this was the day, the jury came back with a "not guilty" verdict for Snoop and his bodyguard. He wasn't sure which way it was going to go, and he was so thankful when the jury agreed he wasn't guilty of murder. Everybody was on pins and needles, and I know it was a big turning point in Snoop's life. He was already a good kid, who wanted to do good things in his life, but it's never easy to stay out of trouble when you're from the hood.

Snoop meant to keep everything cool from here on out, though.

Snoop and Malik—the bodyguard who shot the dude, not the Malik I'd talked to earlier—were still in the courtroom and the jury started walking over to both of them, congratulating them. I used to train with Malik back in the day. He's a total badass and deep into martial arts. I didn't even know until that day it was the Malik I knew who shot Philip, the guy who menaced Snoop.

They cut Snoop's ankle bracelet off and it was Snoop's very first day of freedom since after the incident. They had a celebration party at Monty's in Westwood for Snoop. Everyone who was anyone was there, except for Dr. Dre. There were maybe about three hundred people invited, and Suge paid for every one of them. They were bringing out cases and cases of Crystal, and everyone was having a good time. Death Row's attorney, David Kenner, was there, Snoop's family, the Outlaws, Tha Dogg Pound. Kenner got on the stand and gave a speech, and Snoop and Pac got on the stage and started freestyle rapping. Till this day, I wish I had a video camera. Those boys are so talented. They were jammin' to a live band, and it was unbelievable.

When Pac and Snoop got up onstage, I realized I was looking at two of the brightest stars in the business. They're both so amazingly talented, you had to see it to believe it.

Snoop signaled to me, it was time to go. He and Pac had made plans to meet up later at Pac's Wilshire Avenue house. The two of them hung out the rest of the night, talking about everything, and planning things for the future. Snoop actually started living in the Wilshire house after that, in the west wing.

It's a trip when I look back, because it was such an innocent moment in time. I don't know if either of them fully realized how special they were, and as a team, they would have been unbeatable. Suge had them in the palm of his hands.

I went home at four-thirty A.M., with the two of them still awake, talking, getting stoned, dreamin'.

CHAPTER SIX

DR. DRE

I didn't have the opportunity to spend much time with Dr. Dre, the brilliant producer who built the Death Row empire. I was on my way in as he was on his way out, but what I knew of him, I liked.

The first time I met Dr. Dre was at Can-Am, he was being interviewed by Kevin Powell, the former MTV *Real World* blacktivist poet, who was writing for *Vibe* magazine at the time. Kevin got there as scheduled but Dre was late, and like everybody else, he had to wait in the studio's lobby.

He started chitchatting with me, asking me if I liked working for Death Row and how I liked the whole Death Row family. He would eventually interview Pac and Snoop, too, and as it turned out, he mentioned me in the story also. He described me as a big, black, muscular brotha, and mentioned how tight security was. He himself got patted down, which must have surprised him. We didn't fuck around, though. Nobody came through those doors without a pat-down. Like I said before, Suge set the rules, and we abided by them.

Dre showed up eventually, and they did the interview in a back room.

When they were finished, Dre stepped into Studio A, because he had some work to do with Daz on Tha Dogg Pound record. I went back to introduce myself and handed him one of my business cards. I told him if he ever needed any off-duty security, and he couldn't get ahold of anybody, to give me a call and I'd help him out.

My business card has a bodybuilding picture on it, and Dre looked at the photo and said: "Damn . . . you a swoe-ass nigga."

"Swoe" is slang for *swollen*.

He looked at the photo again and said: "Damn, homie, I'll definitely be giving you a call because I'm always going somewhere at the last minute, and I may decide I need security."

I told him I'd help him out and he could either call Wrightway to hook it up or he could call me directly, and we'd work together.

Dre said, "Hell, I'm not calling Wrightway. I'll call you direct."

Wrightway, of course, wouldn't have been cool with that, but fuck it, I knew what the artists were getting charged and what I was getting paid, and I could save this brotha some money if he worked with me directly.

"Give me them digits, nigga," said Dre, and I wrote them down on the back of my business card.

He pulled up in his white S500 Mercedes, sitting on 20-inch Lorenzers, and I knew this brotha had bank.

I also began to suspect things weren't too straight between him and Suge; there'd been some grumbling but nothing specific. It was coming, though.

The next time I saw Dre was in the city of Orange, California, when we were shooting the video for "California Love, Part 2." It was shortly after Pac got out of jail, and their relationship seemed to be cool, but even if you watch the video now, you can tell Pac wasn't real down with Dre. You can see there's something missing.

Nevertheless, they were working together that day, and we were at this mansion owned by the guy who used to own Clothestime. It was a big old house, and it was so sweet. There were a ton of extras, and they all were in the video. Dre remembered me and just like the first time, he was totally cool with me.

I'll never forget this, though. That day, I was wearing some black Guess? jeans, and my legs are big, there's no way around it. I don't dress myself to draw attention to my physique, but when I'm in competitive shape, it's hard not to notice.

Dre was sitting in this hallway with a girl, and he was pretty fucked-up already. I guess he'd been drinking like everybody else that day. He turned to me and said: "Damn homie, you's a big-ass fucking hamhock. But you gotta get rid of them tight-ass jeans."

He clowned me in front of the girl—I knew exactly what he was doing—but I laughed and shot back with: "Yeah, homie, this is 250 pounds of pure chocolate, too." I was clowning back, switching a line from "Keep Their Heads Ringin'," that talked about "180 pounds of pure chocolate," or something like that.

Dre was cool, he had to have something to clown about because when you're making a video, it's generally boring as shit. You gotta be on the set real early and it usually doesn't wrap until well into the morning. For this one, we worked about nine A.M. till two-thirty A.M. There were exceptions, such as Pac's "How Do U Want It" video, the sex version. Time just flew by on that one, for some reason.

Anyway, Pac and Dre seemed cool with one another that day. Didn't seem to be any problems, to speak of. It wasn't like they were real tight, but it wasn't like the shit that was gonna fly next. All I know is, I began noticing Dre was never around anymore. Whenever there was a Death Row function, Dre would be noticeably absent and I never saw him in the studio anymore. I asked one of the other security guards why Dre was never around and he said, "Dre's got his own studio at his house." I thought, *Yeah, I can see that,* but it still seemed a little strange because he was a part of the family.

Time continued to pass, and I started to hear the studio scuttlebutt. I was on duty one night, and Danny Boy came in—he's a Death Row artist who's an R&B singer with an amazing voice. Like the rest of the Death Row posse, he's real talented.

I saw him enter the studio and said, "What up, D. B.?"

"Ah nothing man," he said, and then added: "That punk-ass mutha-fucka Dr. Dre."

I was like, "Wha . . ."

"Man, you ain't heard?"

I shook my head, "No."

"Gay-ass Dre . . ."

I looked at him like he was crazy.

I said: "Where you hear this from?"

He just shook his head.

Danny was the first one I heard it from, but then after that, I kept hearing shit about Dre. I'm this kind of person, though: I didn't see it, I don't believe it. I don't know nothing about it until more than just one or two people are talking about it.

It continued to heat up. Then they had a meeting, and the meeting was about Dr. Dre. The point of it was this: Death Row was disappointed that Dre never showed up for any of Snoop's trial appearances. He didn't show up when they had the party celebrating Snoop's "not guilty" verdict at Monty's. Something was funny about the whole thing. Dre's definitely the dopest producer in rap, and you'd think Death Row wouldn't want to lose him.

I didn't know what this was all about, so later on, when I got to know Pac better, I asked him about Dre one day. "What's up with Dre, man, I thought y'all was kinda tight," I asked.

"Fuck Dre," he said. "Dre didn't support his homeboy, and he's supposed to be part of Death Row, and he's not even down."

After that, I continued to hear Pac bad-mouthing Dre, and if you listen to "Toss It Up," from the *Makaveli* album, you can hear how serious Pac was about Dr. Dre. In his last interview, he talks about how he was the Don and Suge was the Boss. This came out of Tupac's own mouth.

I listened to him and Suge on the topic once. We were in Vegas at Suge's mansion, before a Tyson fight and I heard Pac tell Suge if he ever saw Dre he was gonna fuck him up. There was a whole lotta bad blood and bad feelings. I can tell you this, it didn't add up to me, that they would turn their backs on Dre because he didn't got to Snoop's trial. If you look at the mathematics of the equation it don't add up, because he's a dope-ass producer. So why now? My guess is, something deep went down between Dre and Suge that caused the split and the rumors were sent out there to publicize the rift, in a way Suge was comfortable with. Dre was always cool with me. Nothing but polite and cordial. He never acted one way or the other.

Whatever caused the split, it was definitely something personal. No doubt about it, something personal was going on between Dre, Suge, and Tupac. Now one of them is dead, another's in jail, and the third guy ain't talking.

I watched interviews with Dre and he never said anything about the problems with Death Row. He always said he had love for Snoop, and it was never a matter of not being down.

Here's a fact, though, which most people don't know. Dre was given a choice, and the choice was this: Leave Death Row either walking out, or get dragged out. When it comes to business, Suge didn't fuck around.

Make no mistake about it, Dre chose to go out walking and no one knows what, if anything, he had to forfeit for this choice. He had to start all over again, and do you think that decision was easy? Hell no. But it's the only choice he could make.

Here's how twisted things got around there. Danny Boy was the closest artist to Suge in some respects. At one point, Reggie told me Danny Boy wanted Suge to adopt him. Reggie apparently told Danny Boy he was crazy, pointing out that his father was still alive.

Danny had finished his album, he had thirty songs ready to go. Death Row, however, never released the album. They released one single, "Slip N Slide," and they also shot a video for it in Cancún, Mexico. The video played a couple of times on The Box, the all-request video channel, and that was it. It just slipped and slid away out of view.

I don't know why they never released the record but it could be because Death Row didn't want to have its first bomb on its hand. I have a copy of the record, and the truth is, it ain't that good. Danny Boy can sing his ass off, but the album is pretty weak. Who knows what their reasoning was, but whatever it was, Danny Boy's relationship with Death Row was not what it was, and that's not a situation you want to be in.

On the other hand, Dr. Dre made Death Row a lot of money, and he still didn't want to be in a situation with Suge. My guess is Dre had outgrown the gangsta thug lifestyle Death Row was living.

I just want Dre to know that just because Death Row had a beef with him, doesn't mean I had a beef with him. I always liked his music and I know he's a down brotha. Shit, I ain't mad at him. If you look at the situation now, you can see who the smart brotha is. Whether he left money behind that was rightfully his or not, Dre got out. He's in a better place than Death Row.

For Tupac, it was just the beginning.

PART THREE

TUPAC SHAKUR

CHAPTER SEVEN

PAC

I was home one night in December, shortly after the New York trip, when Reggie rang me up. "Me and Cedric were talking," he said. "He told me I should call you first."

Cedric was my buddy from the Marines who got me the job, and I wondered what this was about.

"Would you want to bodyguard Tupac?" he asked.

"When?"

"Starting tomorrow."

Tupac, I thought to myself. I had to think about this one. I didn't know the brotha well at this point, and like I said before, what little I knew, I didn't necessarily like. "You know Reggie, right now, I'm gonna say no. But let me get back with you later."

"I need someone for tomorrow, Frank."

"Well, my answer right now, since you need someone for tomorrow, is no, right now."

I called up Kenneth, Cooper, and my boy, K. J. I called K. J. because he'd been Pac's limo driver. I called Kevin Hackie because he'd been bodyguarding him, so had Cooper and Kenneth.

Cooper told me: "I think some of the wildness is out of him right now. You'll be okay. When I first got with him, we were going everywhere. All times of day and night. Just be careful, and make sure you got a full tank of gas."

I asked him why.

"Because he loves to drive fast, and he does not obey the law." I did a little research on him myself, and found out about his life and his recent altercations. His troubled history is well known: He was raised by a single mom, a Black Panther—Afeni Shakur—who as part of the New York 21, was pregnant with him while in prison—the experience he documents in one of his most powerful singles, "Dear Mama," and the only song of his I was familiar with before we started working together. He'd starred in such films as *Juice* and *Poetic Justice*, while all the time getting into his share of trouble. The eight months at Riker's Island was from a 1995 conviction on two counts of sexual abuse stemming from a 1993 incident involving a female fan in a Manhattan hotel room. In 1992, he was involved in a scuffle that resulted in a stray bullet killing a six-year-old boy. The following year he was charged with shooting at two off-duty police officers but the charges were later dropped. On November 30, 1994, he was shot five times during a robbery in the lobby of a Manhattan recording studio—a shooting he believed was a setup coming from Biggie Smalls.

Aside from the trouble that seemed to follow him around, was the weed issue. Very seldom did we ride with the artists, because possession of weed was a big problem. I remember riding around with Tha Dogg Pound, and they were getting fucked-up. They got a kick out of us rolling our windows down, they were fuckin' with us, and we'd fuck with them back. We'd turn the air-conditioning all the way up, or blast the heat on. One time, I opened up the sunroof, and Nate Dogg and Kurupt had a fuckin' heart attack. I didn't want to be inhaling secondary smoke on the job, and they didn't want the smoke to escape.

Nate was yelling, "Close the roof! I wanna party with some of you niggas, now! I know some of y'all get high!" He was talking to security.

Actually, sometimes the relationship reminded me of my jailing experience, especially the visiting days. When we'd fuck with the inmates, they'd fuck with us back. In a way, the situation was similar because we were the cops, trying to keep these boys in line, and to them, we were the security they'd try to outrun.

Pac was at the front of the pack. Before he began working with me, he was legendary for losing security. No one could tell this boy what to do. No one ever wanted to ride in a limo with Pac because if you had a problem with something he was doing, forget it. You weren't gonna tell him anything. Ironically, I actually ended up riding with Tupac a lot, when we would go to court. He went to court stoned, he didn't care. Before he'd brush his teeth, he'd smoke some weed. It's safe to say, Snoop and Pac never showed up for one of their court dates *not* under the influence.

K. J. offered me the best insight on Pac. He used to tell me all the crazy places they'd go to, but he still wanted to be Pac's personal driver so I asked him what was up. "I would do it," said K. J. without hesitating. He told me Pac was basically a good person with a wild streak, but he didn't think it was anything I couldn't handle, provided I didn't mind rolling with someone in gang-related areas who casually wore $50,000 of jewelry and at all times had about five grand in his pocket.

I decided to call Reggie back, and laid out this proposition for him. "Who you got bodyguarding Pac right now?" I asked.

"Kevin, Leslie, Cooper, and Kenneth."

"Okay, that's four guys. Why don't you rotate us, two days on, throughout the week. If you're willing to do that, then I'll work with him. But I don't want it to be every day."

Lori had already started giving me shit about it, and you can't blame her. If I was going to be with him every day, then my life was gonna be with him. It was a difficult decision for me to make because I felt like I had to make a choice between work and marriage. So I tried the compromise and Reggie agreed to give it a try. He'd see how a rotating schedule worked out, and that's what we did for the next few weeks.

I began doing double shifts in the studio and I worked with Pac on Wednesdays and Thursdays. I thought everything was cool, but Kevin and Leslie got into a bickering fight over what days they wanted. They finally got it all worked out, and everybody ended up with two days apiece.

My first full-time shift with Tupac began at the studio. I relieved Leslie up at Can-Am, and worked with Pac until five A.M. I told Pac to notify me when he was ready to go to the hotel, and that I'd be up at the front of the studio. He was staying at the Peninsula Hotel in Beverly Hills that night, or morning as it turned out.

Somewhere around five-thirty A.M., he walked out and didn't say shit to me. The other security guard who was working that night in the camera room, said to me, "Hey Frank, your principal is leaving."

I jumped up, caught up with him, and said, "Do you want me to follow you, Pac?"

"Yeah, just follow me back to the hotel."

He went to his room and told me he'd give me a call when he was ready to leave.

I asked if he knew what room I was in.

"Yeah, it's the room all you niggas stay in."

The next morning, sure as shit, he told me to meet him in the lobby in fifteen minutes.

I went down to the lobby as quickly as I could roll, and there was Pac in the valet area, just about to get into his car. Without a doubt, he was about to leave. He didn't wait for anyone.

I knew exactly what he was up to, though. It was my first day and he was testing me. *Cool,* I thought. *Let him.* I jumped in my car and followed him to do an MTV interview he had with Bill Bellamy, that took place at the Hotel Nikko in Beverly Hills. I was driving my 300ZX that day, and when I pulled up behind him at the hotel, he said to me: "Damn, look at the bodyguard, muthafucka got a car sweeter than mine. Y'all must be getting paid good."

I look at him, like, *Yeah, right.* He didn't know anything about me yet.

What's funny was, the ride over, sure as shit. He hit every yellow light turning red and gunned it, trying to lose me. I followed him on surface streets in and around town at about 50 miles an hour. I had no problem keeping up with him. I had a car that could keep up with his Mercedes, and that's something I'm sure he liked about me right away. He couldn't shake me. Leslie had this old pickup truck, and it couldn't keep up with Pac's cars.

Everything was cool that day. Bill Bellamy said to Pac when he saw me, "Damn, that your bodyguard?"

Pac giggled and said, "Nah, I'm his bodyguard." That ended up being a running joke.

We had no problems, no run-ins. He met with the producer and director of *Gridlock'd,* and later on, his buddies Psych and Bogart met up with us at the Ivy, the trendy restaurant featured in *Get Shorty.* When we got up to leave, Pac was talking about the movie, and he was excited about it.

Man, we packed so much shit into that day. It was definitely a sign of things to come. Not until much later, did I understand why that boy was so driven to do the things he did. I remember being sick as a dog that day with a head cold, but I survived it.

After all the interviews and meetings were done, we went back to the Peninsula and just chilled.

*   *   *

The next day, he had a day off, and all we did was play. He went to the Oakwood Apartments where the Li'l Homies lived, in the San Fernando Valley not far from Can-Am. Damn, this was the stinkiest apartment. It was small, maybe only a two-bedroom pad, and Tupac was paying for everything. They were gettin' high and chillin'—I look back now and think, *If I only knew what was to come. . . .*

We went upstairs on the rooftop of the building, it was actually the top of the parking structure, and they played basketball for hours. Tupac loved to play ball, and I enjoyed watching them. I look back now and wonder if he was trippin' over the fact I wasn't trying to mingle with him. I could've played ball if I wanted to, but I chose to hang back. I think he was used to people—at that point in his career—trying to see what they could get from him. I didn't look at things that way.

He was such a kid, and I'm sure the Outlaws brought it out in him, too. As soon as they got bored with basketball, the next thing they wanted to do was go shoot paint guns. We found this place, way off the Ventura Freeway, and they all went out and shot at each other with paint balls. I hung back in the Surburban with Big Syke, and watched them have fun. They played from about three P.M. until it was dark, and when they finished, they were still so excited. They decided it was gonna be their new sport, and they wanted to buy a shitload of gear.

I know the reason they dug it so much, too. It's because they were shooting guns.

CHAPTER EIGHT

THE CHOSEN ONE

For all his talking and clowning and bragging and craziness, Tupac was quiet when it came to his business. He handled his business in ways that only he knew. Only Pac understood what was going on in his head with the decisions he was making. Until he voiced them, and let everybody else in, he didn't say a word. He was very private about a lot of shit, and only after we began working together one-on-one and forming a tight-knit friendship, did I begin to understand this about him.

For example, I didn't know Tupac was checking me out, considering me for his full-time bodyguard. He must've been observing from a distance and once he made his decision, that's when he told Reggie about it. After we'd been rotating his security for a while, and Tupac had the chance to work with five different bodyguards, he decided out of the five brothas, he wanted to work with me. He'd gotten tired of the switching around, and wanted someone he was comfortable with.

Out of the blue, he told Reggie one day, "I just want one muthafucka, and I want Frank."

I was in Vegas when the word came down. It was March 12, and Reggie called me. "I got good news and bad news," he said. "Which one you want to hear first?"

I said, "It don't matter, because I'm gonna hear them both anyway, so just give me the news."

"The good news is, we just had a meeting."

"Who had a meeting?"

"Suge, Tupac, and me," he said.

I was curious, because obviously the meeting had something to do with me.

"Tupac wants you, and only you, as his permanent bodyguard."

"What brought that on?"

"I have no idea," said Reggie. "I got a phone call from Suge, and he told me to come to the office, we had the meeting, and that was that. Tupac was very specific. He didn't want Kevin Hackie. He didn't want Leslie, he didn't want Kenneth or anybody else. He agreed to using Kevin Hackie on your days off, but that's it."

I didn't hesitate this time. I said yes, right off the bat.

Oh yeah—and the bad news? I would still be getting the same money.

I ran into Pac later that night at 662. He was pulling into 662, with the top down on his new Rolls-Royce. "Hey Frank," he said. "Didn't you get the news?"

It was the night of the Tyson-Bruno fight.

"You gonna be my number one security. I don't want nobody else but you . . . it's gonna be a'ight though—we gonna have some fun."

I thought about his decision and realized he'd spent enough time on the rotation schedule to size everybody up. Or, in Pac's mind, to find faults.

He didn't want to work with Kenneth because Pac felt Kenneth showed fear at the House of Blues incident, when some gangbangers were getting into it with Muta, one of Pac's Outlaws. All of the Outlaws were badass ghetto kids from New Jersey, and they were always getting into trouble. We had more trouble with them than with Pac, but he loved those guys and did everything for them. He gave them a place to stay, he bought them clothes, and the new Suburban. They wouldn't have had anything if it wasn't for Pac.

In this incident, Muta was about to get his ass killed and Kenneth wanted them all out of there. Crips came up, brandishing weapons and said, "What's up, who you with?" Pac wasn't with anybody, but being down with Suge pretty much meant being down with Bloods. There was no getting around it. Pac told the dudes, he was neutral. "I'm just a rapper," he said. They said alright, cool, and let it slide, but Muta wasn't letting it slide. He got into it. Pac knew what was going on, but he didn't run from anything, he didn't back down, he was ready to die for his boy.

So Kenneth, who was doing the right thing in his mind, said, "Hey, Pac, this is an unsafe situation, I think we need to get out of here. The muthafucka's got a gun."

Pac turned to him and said, "You've got a gun, too, nigga, so what's the problem?" He interpreted Kenneth's reaction as cowardice, and Pac didn't want to hear that shit. "Fuck that," he told him, and he never forgave him for it.

The next day, I was working with Pac and he told me the whole entire story. "Punk-ass muthafucka wanted to run," he said. "He's got a gun, so what's the problem? He supposed to be a cop. Yeah, well I tell you what, I don't want that muthafucka bodyguarding me."

Of course, when I spoke with Kenneth, the story was a little bit different. Pac took his actions as a sign of fear rather than concern for his own safety.

With Leslie, it had to do with Pac's personal belief that Les was more into the ladies than he was into watching over Pac.

Basically, he found something he didn't like about everyone in security except me. It was cool, because as much as he was sizing me up, I sized him up, and realized I liked hanging with Tupac Shakur. I liked the shit he was creating and I liked what I did. The truth is, it only took me one day around him to determine it would be easy for me to work with him. By the end of that first shift, I knew I liked the young brotha. I saw the way he behaved with his Li'l Homies, and the way he handled himself in business, and he seemed cool with me.

I was just down, I'm a down brotha. I got a job to do, and I did it and that's that. We just clicked. It's interesting, because when he made the decision I don't think he really knew me all that well, but a few things got his interest. First of all, the situation with Snoop; he took my actions as a sign of courage, the fact I walked into the trailer with my gun brandished, looking for Snoop, and that I wouldn't let the cops push us around. Secondly, we had an incident where I was present at the Le Montrose.

He was looking to hook up with Total and he heard Faith was in town (there's more to this story in chapter 13), and he said, "Let's go to the Spot," his pet name for Le Montrose hotel in West Hollywood.

When his boys, Muta and Yak, started getting into it in front of the hotel, I flew down the stairs and began sizing up the situation. They were out looking for bitches to pull up in limos, and they started jockin' these two women. A limo pulled up, the dude who was with the women got into a beef with the Outlaws. I saw the whole thing go down from the balcony and before anyone could think twice, I was already out the door, talkin' about "Let's hit it." He followed me down the stairs, and was ready to start swinging at this muthafucka. I'm saying to him, "Nah, nah, nah. This dude's a skinny muthafucka and he's alone, let's just see what's going on here."

Turned out Pac knew the dude and everything was handled, but he liked what he saw in me, because Tupac was a warrior, straight up. He walked into flames, not away from them. Whether it was for his own good or not, he didn't care. It was in his blood. For better or worse, I suppose it's in mine, too.

As usual, the fight ends and Pac starts clowning with his boys. The clowning and the braggin' were a part of the package. "Big muthafuckin' Frank, hit the stairs and all you stupid muthafuckas ran to the elevator . . ." he kept clowning them.

That wasn't the only time Pac saw me in action. Another altercation had broken out when we were filming the video for "To Live and Die in L.A." at the Crenshaw Mall in South Central L.A. Some punk kids were hanging out at the mall and they were fuckin' with Pac. He turned around to go at one of 'em and I said to him, "Pac, c'mon, these are just kids."

Then somebody threw something at us.

I turned around, and Pac saw me turn around. He went to rush this muthafucka, but before he could do anything, I dropped a drink I had in my hand and shoved the guy as hard as I could, pushing him back into the crowd.

I hear Pac from behind me, going, "Damn, man, you always fuckin' getting in my way." He was joking about it. "I never fuckin' get a chance to do nothing because you always fuckin' jump in!"

I looked at him, and said, "Well, that's what I am. I'm a body guard. I'll keep you out of trouble, I'll be the one to get into trouble. I'll handle the situation."

We walked back over to the trailer, and he started in with the Li'l Homies.

"Where the fuck was y'all at?! We got into another fight at the mall, there was these li'l niggas, and y'all should been in there fighting! These niggas were y'all ages. Fuckin' big-ass Frank, muthafuckin' Rottweiler, Pit Bull Frank, again, jumps in the middle of this shit. You a fuckin' Rott-weiler."

At the time, I had a Rott named Snoop. Now I got two, God bless 'em. They're the greatest dogs. It was funny because Pac had no idea I liked the breed. Truth is, we had lots in common.

Anyway, Pac got all the homies worked up, and they were ready to go back to the mall.

I said to them, "Fuck y'all, they gone now."

We were in the trailer and were getting ready to shoot an outdoor scene, driving around the neighborhood in a convertible.

Pac wouldn't cut 'em any slack, though. He kept at 'em. "Y'all supposed to be with me everywhere I go. When I leave the trailer, y'all supposed to be on the set. When I go somewhere, y'all supposed to be in the background so when shit like this jumps off, you can handle it. Frank can't fuckin' see everything."

He made a hobby out of shaking his bodyguards before he met me. He tried to in the beginning, but he stopped once he realized he couldn't shake me. As he got to know me better, I took him aside and laid it out for him.

"Pac, you can't be shaking me. You shake me, and you'll get into some trouble if you don't have a credible witness. You shake me, something happens, we're both in trouble." He took the advice to heart, and the only time he ever lost me when we were out in public was the day of his murder. Till this day, I sometimes wonder why I was the chosen one. I can only speculate. Pac held the answer to that question; now only God knows, and when I see Pac again, I'll know.

The more I was around him, however, the more I started noticing all the characters inside him. In the true sense of the word, he was a clown, a total comedian. To know him was to like him. I used to tell him all the time, he missed his calling. He was so fuckin' funny. Not a day went by when I was working with him, when he didn't make me laugh. His dangerous side was every bit as strong as his funny and lovable side, which definitely made things interesting. This contradiction stressed a lot of people out, but it didn't stress me out. I sort of understood it, and he wasn't directing the shit at me.

CHAPTER NINE

DEATH AROUND THE CORNER—GETTIN' PAID

From the time I started working with Pac until the time of his death, I watched him accomplish more in one year than most people do in a lifetime. The moment he got out of prison, he went straight to Can-Am and banged out "All Eyez on Me," his first recording for Death Row, and a double album no less. My buddy K. J. says he did the first six tracks in one night. All the while, he's shooting videos and flying to awards shows.

When he finished that record, we went on tour, performing around the country with Tha Dogg Pound. He was already working on his next record, *The Don Killuminati: The Seven Day Theory*, under the Makaveli pseudonym, which Death Row released right after his death. We began working on the movie *Gridlock'd*, a dark comedy about two junkies who are trying to kick, and that's when the pace really began to pick up. We were shooting about one video a week, while the movie was still in production. Sometimes, the videos would run two days, and he'd be doing double-duty with *Gridlock'd*. I would literally be on the set of the film from seven A.M. to seven P.M. and we'd wrap and drive straight to a video shoot, then finish the video, and it'd be time to head back to *Gridlock'd*.

The videos we made during this time were "Toss 'Em Up," "Made Niggaz," "Hit 'Em Up," and "To Live and Die in L.A." In the middle of all this, he recorded the albums *One Nation* and *Outlaw Immortals featuring Tupac*, sometimes in the dead of the night, and this when he wasn't shooting videos. He completed both records.

People used to ask me, "How the fuck are y'all doing it?" I said, "We're just doing it."

At the time, I didn't stop to think about why he was working so much. At first, I figured, *That's just Tupac.* He used to write songs in the trailer that he would record later that night. If something came to him, he scribbled it down then drove to the studio when we left the set. He was amazingly fast, he'd record a new song in a matter of hours. He didn't fuck around.

One time, we were driving in the limo, we'd just come from a court appearance . . . Oh yeah, there were a lot of those. Half the time, he couldn't even keep track of what the hearings were about, he had so many suits against him. Most of the time, it was related to a gun possession or a fight, pending cases, probation hearings. Anyway, the drive to and from court must have inspired him because I remember Tupac saying, "Tell the limo driver to pull over, Frank."

So the driver did, and Pac jumped out of the car and into a store. He came out with a handful of ballpoint pens and a spiral notepad. By the time we got back to his house, he'd written a song. He did that all the time. He wrote music real fast, he knew what was in his head.

When we finished *Gridlock'd* we flew to Italy for a week, and then he spent the month of August making the movie *Gang-Related*.

No one seemed to know what was up with him. Tupac probably didn't even know why he was doing it. He was driven like no one I'd ever met before. At first, I thought he was making up for lost time, the time lost in prison. As I look back now, I think he must have had premonitions, either conscious or unconscious, of his death. No one was cracking a whip on him, it was all self-inflicted. He was getting everything done that he could possibly do, as well as starting up his own record label and production company. The wheels were rolling on both those projects. He was definitely on some mission.

There's little question part of his burning ambition might have been to be finished with his three-record contract with Death Row. He was so talented and only really needed Suge in the beginning, when he was willing to post $1.5 million bail to get him out of Riker's. Once he was out and had gotten on his own two feet again, he was ready to take on a world that would've eventually been bigger than that of Death Row Records.

Whether he sensed his own destiny or not, he was definitely a man with a plan. Part of why we clicked was a shared mutual respect for each other's professionalism. I can't say what Tupac was like before prison, but when I worked with him, he behaved like a professional. I watched him pour his heart out into *Gridlock'd*, because he had so much pressure on him to not fuck up that movie like he'd done in the past. He overcame his reputation, and every day I saw this guy killing himself to make that movie, to do videos, to make more music. By choice, he put the pressure on himself, he wanted to change his reputation, and wanted to be thought of as a true professional. To see him perform was to be watching history. I got off on the way other people would trip when they saw him in action, whether it was the energy he put into a video or behind the mike. It was raw and it was brilliant, and you could see it.

You just had to have been there. From the first day he began filming the movie *Gridlock'd* I knew a lot of people on the set had preconceived ideas about Pac. True to form, once they got to know him, they all fell in love with him. Tim Roth, the actor who was starring as Tupac's partner, became real close with Pac. The producer and director also got attached to him. I would hear people on the set talking about it all the time, "Hey, this guy's a fuckin' alright guy." People started coming up to me, and saying, "I didn't know Pac was cool like that." Everyone was impressed and some people even seem shocked that this controversial brotha was so professional. He showed up each day on time, he was always prepared, he made people laugh, and he was just cool.

The thing is, he expected the same from everyone around him. If Tupac didn't like a person he was working with, forget it. They were outta there. He fired this one production assistant on the set of the "Hit 'Em Up" video.

"I don't want that stupid bitch around me," he said, and that's it, she was gone.

She was a stupid bitch, too. She was trying to be helpful but she didn't know what she was getting herself into. During the filming, she returned Pac's pager calls, and asked the person on the other end who was calling and what it was concerning. When she handed the phone over to Pac, it was clearly one of his women, who wanted to know who the fuck was asking who she was. Pac called the girl over to him when he hung up the phone, and said, "Did you answer my pager?" She said yes.

"Why did you question who was on the other line? If someone calls and asks for Tupac, you just give me the phone. Don't worry about who's calling me, because if I didn't want them to call, they wouldn't have my number."

He got really upset about it, but he cut her some slack, he liked the owner of the production company, and she was trying so hard to be efficient and wanted to do a lot of work in the future with Pac.

Then she did something really fucked. He left his pager in the trailer when he left the set one night. She was cleaning up for him, so the trailer would be nice and tidy when he returned the next day. The pager went off, and what does she do? She calls the number on the pager, and again, it was one of his women.

The person finally got ahold of Tupac and said, "Hey, I paged you, and some chick answered the page." He said, "How? I have my pager . . ." When he went to look for it, he realized it was gone.

The next day, when we returned to the set, he called her over and asked if she had his pager.

"Oh yeah, I found it," she said.

Tupac completely lost it. He was screaming at her, yelling at her to get the fuck out of his trailer. Poor girl didn't know what hit her. She wasn't doing it on purpose. I had a long talk with her, because I had to calm her down, and I explained, "That's Tupac, you don't go answering someone else's pager. You don't answer someone's phone and question people. He's trying to give you a job, and you're fucking up."

She didn't work with Tupac anymore, but he kept working with the production company. It's called Look Hear Productions. The owner is a woman named Tracy, and she really went through the ringer herself with Death Row. She got death threats and a lot of shit went down on her end. Tupac liked her a lot and wanted to start a production company with her. He was going to finance it and let her run it. But Suge didn't like that at all. Remember, the way Suge looked at things was, he was the only one who was gonna be making any money.

She's alright now, but the feelings still linger.

He even got mad at Snoop over work. We were getting ready to roll to the set of Roseanne's late-night show, Tupac and Snoop were scheduled to perform "Two of America's Most Wanted," when Pac got a call. When he got off the phone, he stood up, flicked his Newport and said, "Fuck . . . now this muthafucka's not even gonna show up." Snoop flaked at the last minute, and it probably had something to do with an incident between the two of them in Cabo. Snoop lost his dog, Killer, after his girlfriend put the dog on a leash and the dog tried to jump off the balcony. It hanged itself, and Snoop went into a state of depression. He wouldn't go into the studio and he was hurting over it. Killer was a red pit and it was the prettiest little dog you could imagine. Pac couldn't understand it. They were doing a lot of shit together and Pac didn't understand how Snoop could let it get in the way of work.

Ice T was hosting the show that night, and Pac switched the duet he was supposed to have done with Snoop to "Only God Can Judge Me," and he rocked it. Later on, he and Ice T did a crazy duet of "You Don't Bring Me Flowers," a ballad that Barbra Streisand sang with Neil Diamond. It was really funny and it came off great, but nobody knows this. He hated it. Pac was so embarrassed about singing that song. The whole way back he complained about it.

All I know is, Tupac wasn't easy to work with, but for some reason, he and I worked well together. I think I made a point of trying to understand him, rather than simply reacting to his temper. Most of the time he was courteous to people, and time and time again he'd prove how generous his heart was. He also had a forgiving heart, he wasn't the type of person who made his mind up and something was final. I'd hear him fly off the handle at people he was close with, and then become accepting and forgiving. I also heard him apologize a few times.

When we were working on *Gridlock'd* I waited on him hand and foot and he always thanked me. I'd make sure they had food in the trailer for him: he loved soul food, and his favorite food was Buffalo chicken wings. All the other stars had catered food and I felt he should have the same. I just wanted him to be well cared for. He appreciated what I did for him.

It was hot as fuck during the time we worked on the movie, and he let me stay in the trailer with him. I was there as much as I wanted and didn't have to knock. Anybody else who came in that door, had to knock. Other security guards, production assistants, whatever, they all had to rap on the door.

One time, Kevin came in to kick it with me and Pac gave me this look, which meant, *You and your homeboy get the fuck out of here*. I could read him and I got the message. Later on, when I returned, he told me, "Look,

Frank, you know I don't care if you're in the trailer, but I don't want Kevin in here, or Leslie. You the only nigga who can come in the trailer. If you're gonna bring your homies in with you, stay out."

Rather than react and be hurt or angry, I simply took it for what it was worth. He wanted to concentrate on his shit; he was, after all, making a movie. While he didn't mind having me around, he wasn't looking for an entourage.

He once told me he liked the fact I knew how to turn on and turn off. I was the only one in his mind who knew how to kick it like one of the guys, but when it came down to clicking back on to work, it was no problem. I didn't blur the lines.

I had prior experience in bodyguarding, and knew what lines not to cross. Kash knew that I knew A to Z about him, and he already had problems trusting people. I had this little black book that was nearly full of names of his women, and I knew all his business, and handled it for him. He got to the point, where he started to distrust me. I would never have betrayed his trust, it's just in my blood. I have morals, and where I come from, loyalty is everything. I kept trying to tell Reggie that, but he wasn't hearing it.

I told Kash that, too. Unfortunately, neither of them could believe that loyalty actually existed to the degree it did in me.

Where I come from and where Tupac comes from, loyalty is everything. From the earliest days of working with him, I knew he would eventually want to get off Death Row. Privately, I was waiting for the right time to hit him up to work without Wrightway. I wanted to let him know I was down for him, and fuck all the D.R. bullshit. Larry told me what the artists were getting charged and Tupac didn't need to pay middleman fees to Wrightway.

Tupac once told me his maid made $200 every time she cleaned his house, and she cleaned his house three times a week.

I couldn't believe it. I asked him to tell me again how much she makes, and when he did, I just shook my head and said, "Guess what I'm getting paid for bodyguarding? Here it is, I'm protecting your life and I'm getting paid what your maid gets paid. That's fucked-up, isn't it?"

He said, "Yeah, you need to talk to Suge about that. We need to get you a pay raise."

I never said a word to Suge but Pac must have, because soon after,

Suge came around the set of *Gridlock'd* and approached me. He asked me how Pac was doing. I told him he was on time, he knew his lines, everything was cool.

Suge looked at me, and said, "I'm glad you and Pac get along, 'cause he really likes you. And I'm glad that you're his bodyguard. We need to get with Reg, and talk about putting you on salary." This was in June of 1996. After that, I told Reggie, and he went through the ceiling about it.

As you'll learn in the next couple of chapters, however, there were other perks to working with Tupac Shakur than mere money.

PART FOUR

THUG LIFE

CHAPTER TEN

CANDY

Tupac had a sweet tooth for candy, but it's not what you're thinking. "Candy," to Pac, was weed, it was his code name for the Chronic, and something he couldn't get enough of. Pac smoked weed 24-7. At first, I didn't know what he was talking about when he used the word *candy*. When we were on a video set or at a film shoot, he would always ask the Outlaws, "How much candy we got left?" I always thought, *Candy? I never seen no candy*. I was thinking jujubes, or Jelly Bellies, and I couldn't figure it out. One day, I approached Pac with a little film canister and said, "Pac, can I get a little bit of your bud?"

He said, "Oh, you mean 'candy'?"

It dawned on me right then, *Aaaahhh, now I get it.*

He gave me one of his little Pac laughs and said, "Yeah, calling it candy is the way we can talk about it with people around but be discreet at the same time. It's a name I came up with." From that time on, there was no mistaking it. The cool thing about working with Pac was, I didn't have to spend any money on it.

Pac loved weed so much, there was no doubt about it. He was also very generous with his stash. If he didn't have any on him, though, you didn't want to be around him. We were at the Le Montrose hotel in West Hollywood one night and Pac realized they were out of candy. He was going literally berserk. "Fuck, I can't believe this shit. We got plenty of drink but no weed!" He was trippin' and I got to thinking, *Who do I know off of Sunset?* and then it hit me. I remembered meeting this dude, in '95, at the Christmas party we'd had the year before. He sold weed to Tha Dogg Pound and that whole crew, and he'd given me his number, because I had some friends I was gonna turn on to it. Lemme just tell you, this was the funkiest-smelling pot I'd ever smelled in my entire life. I first got introduced to this pot when we were shooting "New York, New York." Remember, when I walked into the trailer and, *wooom*, it hit me like a ton of bricks, and they were all screaming, "Close the door, close the door!" They didn't want any of the smoke to escape the trailer. Like true Doggs, they were lapping the smoke up. They wanted to smoke the shit, inhale the secondary smoke, and basically get as fucked-up on it as possible. It stunk so bad. This shit had the worst stench I'd ever smelled. I was like, *Damn, that's pretty funky.*

I saw how fucked-up they were getting, though, and I thought, *Hmmm, maybe when I'm off duty I should try to hook some of that shit up.* Everyone who worked with me knew I never once smoked weed or got fucked up on the job. When I was off duty, though, that was a different story.

This shit was greener than anything I'd ever seen before. No bud looked or smelled like the Dogg Pound dealer's bud. So at the Christmas party, I asked my partner K. I. to introduce us. I asked how much it would cost me if I wanted to hook up with his stash. He told me $75 for an eighth, and I thought, *Shit, that's expensive.* But I remembered the smell, and figured it was probably worth it. I hooked it up and it was unstoppable. We couldn't stop it, it was the wildest weed. I can't compare it to anything I've ever smoked before. I've never done any other drugs besides weed, so I don't know if it's like mushrooms or what, but it was so unstoppable. Man, Tha Dogg Pound really knew their shit when it came to weed. Luckily, I'd made this connection, because this was the only dude I could think of when Tupac was losing it at Le Montrose. This was the weekend he was trying to get with Total, and he didn't want to be without weed.

I flipped through my little organizer, and lo and behold, there was the dude's number. I told Pac, "I know where we can get some weed. You know that nigga, that Tha Dogg Pound be fuckin' with? You want me to hook that up?" He said, "Hell yeah."

I paged him and he called back about ten minutes later.

"Damn, Frankie," said Pac. "You hooked a nigga up."

This was the first time I ever had any dealings with Pac on that level. He was reachin' out to everybody tryin' to get some weed, but it didn't occur to him to ask me. The dealer used to hang out at the studio all the time, he was a white dude, and he knew the score.

I asked Pac how much he wanted and he told me, "Tell him I want a half."

I didn't know what he meant by "a half." So I had to ask him to be specific.

He said, "An O-Z." So I told the dealer, who obviously knew what he wanted and about fifteen minutes later, *voilà*. Dude shows up with a big Ziploc bag, filled to the brim with weed.

They started doing their thing, and everybody was in love again, saying, "My nigga Frank, my nigga Frank . . . hooked it up."

Weed was weed to them, they didn't care how good or how bad it was. When they bought it, though, they only got the best. Why he smoked so much was understandable when you were around him a lot. Weed was a necessity for Pac, without it, he'd lose it. He said it himself on the track, "Lord Knows," from the album *Me Against the World*. He spelled it out:

"I smoke a blunt to take the pain outta me / If I wasn't high, I'd probably blow my brains out, Lord knows."

I think there's truth to that, because when he had his candy, he was straight. It calmed him and relaxed him, and helped his thinking process. Anybody who smokes good bud knows the benefits of it. You see through situations, and you see through people, it acts like a truth serum for a lot of people. For Pac, it was as necessary as brushing his teeth in the morning.

I guess it was a family thing. Whenever I showed up at the Wilshire house, every single time, I'd be sitting with his mom first thing in the morning, and she'd be out there on the porch. I'd walk inside and pot would be all over the coffee table, pot would be everywhere.

When he first got out of bed every morning, he rolled a Philly Blunt. Tupac taught me how to make one. I'd never seen it done before I met him and you basically take a cigar—a Philly Blunt—slice it up the middle like you're gutting a fish, take out the tobacco, and replace it with weed. The shit's so good, you'll never go back once you've been turned on.

Really, for Pac, weed was his drug of choice, it was what he did to relax, and calm down, and get his clock set. In the order of importance, Tupac looked at things like this: Money, first. Weed, second. Pussy, third. That's saying a lot, too, because he really loved women.

Every time we were going to a video shoot or when we were working on *Gridlock'd*, whenever Pac was running short, he'd have me call whoever the production person on the set was to make sure he had pot. They always seemed to know the type of pot he wanted and who to get it from. There was never any question about it and no questions asked. Most of the videos were shot through Look Hear Productions, so they knew what was up.

For the most part, he had as much as needed. When he didn't have it, he didn't turn into a monster or anything like that, but you know how a smoker becomes when he can't find a cigarette? It's the same type of thing. It's just like a nicotine fit. He had those, too. He smoked Newports like he smoked pot.

We used to joke in the studio all the time about how if you took away the alcohol and you took away the weed, these niggas wouldn't be able to rap. Tha Dogg Pound joked about it, too. I remember them messing around one day, saying without weed, half the shit they do would probably sound wack.

Whenever they were working in the studio, they were either stoned or drunk and usually both. I mean fucked-up. There was never a problem about having weed in the studio because every Tom, Dick, and Harry in that studio—except for security and maybe one or two of the engineers— had weed. We searched everybody who came through, and everybody had weed on 'em. We'd pull all kinds of bags out of their pockets, it was everywhere.

For the most part, it was always cool. No one ever fought over weed. There were plenty of fights because of weed, people getting stupid. Just like some people get "liquid courage," ready to take on the world when they're fucked-up, a lot of these characters, they would get "smoke cour- age." Same thing. You got to remember that the more they smoked, the more they drank, too, so it was a combination of drugs.

I gotta say, though, I never saw Tupac get too high or too drunk to handle his business. And this nigga smoked a lot of weed. The closest he came was the last night of the *Gridlock'd* shoot, when he "saw double" and threatened to kick my ass, but even that situation he got under control before he took it too far. Once again, they were keeping the trailer door shut so they could maximize the benefits of the secondary smoke. I don't know, maybe that had something to do with it. He had a little too much in his system.

For the most part, Tupac benefited from the weed he smoked. A lot of people just say, "No, all drugs are bad." But clearly, not all drugs are bad. In fact, in Pac's case, it unlocked a lot of creative channels in his brain, as well as calming him down. It's the same thing for Snoop, and Tha Dogg

Pound, when they get in that state of mind in the recording studio, it sounds more entertaining and more real. They get into the beat even better. Even for me, if I'm watching a movie or listening to some music, I hear it with a clarity I wouldn't normally have. It intensifies your feelings. Tupac lived his life at that level.

During the time I spent with Pac, he probably bought four or five pounds of weed. You figure he was buying for his homies, parties he shared with his mother, his own habit. Traveling with him took serious advance preparation. The only time he didn't take any weed when we traveled was when we went to Europe. He didn't even want to chance it. When Pac was on the plane, he'd just drink Hennessey. That was part of "Thug Passion," the drink of choice. The other drink was Crystal and Alizé; they mixed the two and came up with a fruity passion cocktail. The weed was supposed to be hooked up for him when he landed in Italy, and when he found out it wasn't he freaked out.

When we were traveling within the U.S., though, you can rest assured, weed traveled, too. A lot of times they'd try to get security to carry their bags, but we couldn't touch them. We couldn't be liable, or have to put up with some trumped-up charges. All I can say, is the weed always got to where we were going. No matter what, they worked it out. They'd stick it in their luggage and they never had a problem, it would just fly in with the bags. No dogs ever sniffed the luggage. We never had a problem because we were on domestic flights. If they wanted to bust them, they could have, but then you've got entrapment because they would have been singled out.

Although I never got fucked up on the job, I will say this: Tupac taught me to appreciate weed all over again. I used to smoke weed in high school, but then didn't all through my career in the military and when I worked as a jailer. After I left law enforcement, I smoked weed again on occasion, just for relaxation. Pac figured out I smoked weed the day I paged the dealer at Le Montrose, but he never said anything to me about it one way or the other. He wasn't surprised when I approached him on the subject, though.

I asked him how much he was spending on weed.

He said, "I don't know. I just pay for it, nigga."

I pressed him though, because I was thinking of buying an eighth for myself. "Obviously you don't have the problem I have," I said.

"What's that?"

"I need to find out the price for myself," I said.

"You get stoned, Frankie?" he joked.

I told him I smoked for years, before stopping when I went into the service.

He looked at me, and said, "Go ahead and take some."

I said, "Really?"

Ah yeah, I'm thinking. We were in the trailer on the set of *Gridlock'd*, and I'll never forget how happy I was. From that day on, I never bought it. He'd tell me to help myself whenever it was around. I'd never go near his stash during the day, but when it was close to getting off duty, I'd come around.

One night, when we were at his house in Calabasas, I asked him, "You got anything rolled up?"

He said, "You need something, Frank? Tell the homies to roll you something up."

So I went over to where Malcolm was sitting and asked him to roll me up something.

"Man, how come you never just get stoned with us?" he said.

"Because that's not professional," I told him. "What if something jumps off and I can't handle my business?"

"That's right, that's right," he said. "That's why Pac likes you, man. Because you're professional."

Malcolm hooked me up, and the next time I saw Pac, a couple days later, he hooked me up again. It got to the point where I'd keep an empty film canister on me, and at the end of my shift, he'd tell me to go ahead and fill it up. I would pack that son of a bitch so tight, and when I got home, I would have at least an eighth, plus. He had so much weed on him usually, and he knew I was doing it—he was cool with it. He saw I had a film canister, so it wasn't like I was gonna take a whole lot. It's like, how much can you get in there?

One time I needed some and he wasn't around, but the weed was sitting in the trailer, all laid out. I helped myself because I knew if Pac walked in at that moment, it would be cool. Of course, it's courteous to ask, but with us being tight and it being me, it wasn't an issue. If he walked in, it wouldn't have been like, "Oh shit. . . ." It would've been cool. For the most part, other niggas were smokin' his shit all day long.

We even had a conversation about it. I told him I'd never smoke while

I was on duty, and he said, "I know, nigga, help ya'self." That was that. If you knew Tupac, you knew he was one of the most generous people you'd have the pleasure of meeting. He was the kind of guy who'd give you the shirt off his back. That's if he liked you, of course.

If Tupac liked you, he liked you with passion. If Tupac loved you, he loved you with passion. If he didn't like you, he disliked you with passion. If he hated you, he hated you with passion. There was no middle ground. If he liked you or loved you, he loved you with everything that he was about. The reverse was equally true. He didn't compromise his feelings.

One thing Tupac definitely loved, was women. He loved women, and they loved him back.

CHAPTER ELEVEN

HOOCHIES AND GROUPIES

I couldn't count the number of hoochies Pac slept with while I was working with him. I don't have enough fingers and toes, because it would have to be in the three digits. Suffice it to say, if you were a groupie and you wanted a piece of Pac, chances are, you'd get it. He'd didn't disappoint many fans. Every single video we worked on, he fucked many women on the set. He fucked the extras, the leads, you name it. And we did a lot of videos. As far as movies, it's the same story. In Italy, he fucked three women over there. On the "How Do U Want It" video, he fucked women all that day, and then he had a sex party the last night. Ron Hightower, the porn director, threw an after-party that was really an orgy. He snuck out under a table and went to the party, he didn't want any security that night. Suge, Norris, Roy—shit, nearly every Death Row employee—called me that night looking for him. I knew where he was, and it looked as if he had company, so to speak.

One thing's for sure, Death Row knew how to party. They had orgie parties, sex parties, after-hours shit, postproduction wrap parties—D.R. was all about California Love. The more, the merrier.

Let's just break it down for you. Women threw themselves at Pac, and he wasn't dodging.

Tupac wasn't prejudiced when it came to women. He loved them all. People often stepped to him and said, "Pac, you should only be with black women, because you're a strong black male and you stand for something." Clearly it was Suge's concern, Reggie was just the messenger.

Reggie used to complain to me. "What's up with Pac, he's got all these white girls in his videos? It don't look good."

He was particularly concerned about "How Do U Want It."

I said, "Why don't you just ask him, Reggie."

"You the closest to him, that's why I'm asking you."

"Hey," I said. "That's just what he likes. That's what he wants."

Tupac loved women, period. I don't care if they were black, white, Mexican, Puerto Rican, Chinese, Japanese, it did not matter. He liked pussy. Yeah, he liked paper, meaning he liked cash, he liked his weed, but the one other thing he couldn't live without was pussy. Above my fireplace, I have a signed collage of Death Row photos, and on it, Tupac wrote to me: *To my road dog, big swoe-ass Frank, let's get paper and women—Tupac.*

Ninety percent of the time, that's what he was thinking about. He fucked uncountable women when we were on tour. Brother had stamina. They'd get 'em backstage, after his homies would single them out from the front. Everybody had their own dressing room. It was all laid out. This was in January, and it was Tha Dogg Pound and Tupac. If you went back into the dressing room, and you started partying, smoking pot and doing what they do, you gonna get fucked. You didn't go into that room and not come out unfucked if you're a woman.

Every single video shoot, Tupac fucked a least two women or more. On "How Do U Want It," he fucked so many women he passed out. I couldn't get him to wake up because he was so exhausted. That video shoot was legendary. First off, if you listen to the words of the song, it's all about a baller, a player, who's out macking a bitch. It's about a man who could have any woman he wants and he's talking to the woman he's with that night, asking her how she wants it. At one point in the song, he says, *"Is it cool to fuck? 'Cause I'm not here to talk."*

Leslie remembers him saying that for real when they were on tour with him in Cleveland. He had one of his homies bring these two black girls backstage, and on their way to the hotel, he interviewed them.

"One was on the right of him and one was on the left," says Leslie. "I heard him say, 'So, both of y'all want to come back to my hotel room with me?' They nodded. He said, 'But I'm still confused, it's two of you guys . . .'

"One took him by the chin and kissed him on the lips. When she was finished, the other woman bent over and also kissed him on the lips. " 'Oh, it's like that,' he said. They both started giggling. He said, 'We gonna fuck.' They both looked at him and smiled and started giggling. 'Yeah . . .'

"He said, 'Okay, you know I got to clear that out, because my black ass ain't going back to jail.' "

Both Les and I find it hard to believe Tupac raped anybody. After spending a lot of time with Tupac, I also don't believe he was on some trip where he got off on sexual abuse. The fact is, he got off on women, and they got off on him, and it's difficult to believe he hurt anybody. The truth is, he loved the fuck out of the women. For the most part, the groupies made the approach. They were the ones trying to meet him and get with him. They had their own things in mind. When I think about the charges that got him sent to Riker's, it's like, Why rob a bank, if you have millions?

Tupac's friend, Mike Tyson, hadn't lost his sexual appetite, either, despite his own sexual assault conviction. Tupac and Mike had become close friends ever since Mike sent Pac a letter in prison. He happened to be with us when we were in Cleveland and all it took was a nod for Suge to hook his shit up. Usually, women who hung out around the Death Row camp knew what was up and were just as freaky as the men.

This is how buck-wild things were around there.

During the end of Tupac's set, Tyson came on the stage and asked Les about one of Pac's background dancers. Les ended up mentioning to Suge that Mike liked the dancer, and Suge told her to go get busy. She finished the show and everyone started walking to the back dressing room.

Someone asked where Mike was, and one of the security guards said he's in Tha Dogg Pound's dressing room with this particular dancer, who we all knew.

I was right outside the door because I was working with Tha Dogg Pound at the time, and I was talking to a member of Mike's entourage when she came out of there about twenty-five minutes later, with lipstick all over her face.

I know most of you have probably only seen the "G-rated" version of the "How Do U Want It" video, which is little more than watching a Tupac concert, but there's an X-rated one, too, with topless women everywhere, dancing erotically and spilling champagne on their titties; while Tupac plays with one, another woman's coming up from behind working him. Even the video seems G-rated compared to what really went down that day.

Oh my God, trip off this. The shoot took place over two days, at a club in Hollywood called the Love Lounge. There's a gym downstairs and people were trippin', watching all these porn stars come and go. Most of the girls were either strippers or triple-X stars, straight up. It was a closed set and the producer made everyone take their clothes off. He stripped down, too, and was walking around only in his socks. The freak was on.

Tupac fucked this one chick first. We were all in the trailer listening. When he was done with her, he shot a couple of scenes, finished doing that, and he put his hands around this other girl while another chick was watching—she told me she *really* liked Pac. He was doing it in front of her friend, and they were all getting off on it.

The trailer was rockin'. I was sitting on one end of the trailer, and they were in the back, but you could hear the noises and by the time I looked up, another girl had crawled in with them, and he fucked her, too. He came out of the trailer with a shit-eating grin. He knew all of the girls were friends, because he'd flown them in from Las Vegas. You gotta see these girls, these are some fine fucking girls. This wasn't your run-of-the-mill porn skank—they were fine women. Three times, he walked out of the trailer, shot a scene, got something to eat, came back and started fuckin'.

Now check this out. When he left the trailer for a third time, he made his way out to the set but not without stopping and finger-fuckin' every porn star who was there that day. One star in particular, this woman named Nina Hartley, took his hand and was showing him how to play with a woman's pussy proper. So he tested out Nina's suggestions on any woman who wanted it. The fact is, most of them wanted it. He'd handpicked the women who were on the shoot (no pun intended). A lot of the women were from New York, and they'd flown out specially to be in the video. He didn't fuck around with no dogs, and if you can get your hands on a copy of the X-rated version, you'll see what I'm talking about. It aired on the Playboy Channel, because it was made for Playboy.

A couple weeks later, we shot the concert version, and he fucked two more chicks from that production. I saw one of the women walking into the trailer, she had her makeup all on and looked all done-up. I looked at Kevin and we both said, "Uh-oh." By the time she came out, her lips were all fucked-up. Makeup was everywhere.

*   *   *

Now you know Tupac loved women, but do you know why women loved Tupac? The obvious reasons are his talent, his looks, and his charisma. But he also had a secret arsenal.

I may as well spell it out.

Tupac had a fuckin' horse cock.

The only reason I know this is, at one of Death Row's infamous sex parties, Suge, who flew in bitches from everywhere, brought in forty women from Atlanta. Forty black girls. 4-0. He flew them into Las Vegas. Tupac and I flew in to meet up with them. This was the first time I got to fly first-class with Pac, and it was cool. The limo picked us up, and we went straight to Suge's house. He'd had a party the week before that Tupac didn't go to. That time Suge had flown in women from Ohio. By the time we got to Suge's house, there were maybe four or five still there, cleaning Suge's house. The place was spotless, which was cool because later that night, the front door came open and women started walking in like there was no tomorrow. They just kept coming and coming, and limos kept pulling up with women getting out. I thought to myself, *Damn! These niggas know how to pah-tay!*

The party was catered with the best soul food around, smothered pork chops and smothered chicken, fried chicken, barbecued ribs, collard greens, black-eye peas and rice, cornbread, sweet potato yams, macaroni and cheese, and always more food to go around than what we could eat. One thing I can say about Death Row is we always ate good. Suge hooked it up.

On that night, though, people had other things on their mind. As soon as women start showing up, right away, and I mean right away, the pot gets laid out. Liquor, everywhere, just laid out. People got festive real quick.

At one point, I looked around for Tupac and someone told me he was in another room of the house. I was kickin' it by the television and I was fuckin' around with the remote. I started switching channels. Turned out I grabbed the wrong remote, because when I began flippin' channels, I got a view of one of the bedrooms. Nobody knew this, not even Suge, but one of the bedrooms had a camera in it. Pac was in that room with this chick. He'd hooked up with this light-skinned sister, who had short hair and looked like she might be part Asian. As usual, she was fine. He had her all night, he didn't fuck with any of the other girls.

When I hit on this channel accidentally, I could see Tupac with this girl. I only saw what was happening for a split second. I turned it off right away because I didn't want to invade the brotha's privacy. It wouldn't look cool if a bunch of people were sitting around watching Tupac fuck this bitch.

Later on when Suge showed up, I told him about it. He said, "I don't have any cameras in the bedroom." I showed him the channel and there was nobody in there at the time, and Suge flipped: "No shit! I got fuckin' cameras in the bedroom?" Everybody started laughing when I told them Pac had been in there.

By this time, Pac was already in the shower in what we called "the Red Room," which was Suge's master suite. I walked in, fully clothed, of course—I wasn't a participant. There were a bunch of people in the room and when Pac walked out, he was butt-ass naked and you could see his dick. Pac was chasing this one big muscular bitch with his dick, and ask anybody who was there, brotha had a big dick.

It wasn't like he was trying to hide anything. Since all the women were either dressed in scandalous bikinis or shorts or were walking around nude, they were participating in the orgy that was going on. There wasn't any raping or anything illegal happening. It was consensual sex among adults. Fuckin' went on all night long. It was one big fuck-fest, put on as only Death Row knew how.

There was another one after one of the Tyson fights. The night he fought Frank Bruno. This time, he rented a house out for the occasion. His place wasn't ready yet. It was a house next door to Mike Tyson's. Tyson was invited but he didn't come, and there were even more bitches than the last time.

I'd seen Tupac with some amazing-looking women, women who looked liked they should be with a husband. I watched him dog them out, over and over again. Women threw themselves at Pac and he chose what he wanted and threw the rest back. Brotha didn't just fuck something walking. They definitely had to have a look about them. He favored tits and ass, didn't matter if they were short or tall.

I only remember one time questioning a women he picked up one. She was this white chick and she wasn't anything spectacular. I asked him, "Man, what are you doing with this bitch?" And he said he had nothing better to do that night. It was after a video shoot. The next morning, when

I picked him up, she was there, wearing the same clothes she had the day before. Get this, we see the girl out again at another shoot a few weeks later, and she's wearing the same outfit, again.

I thought, *This is a scandalous girl right here.*

Sometimes his sexual encounters were more innocent. Leslie remembers an incident that took place with only a kiss. He was riding to the Century Club in a limo with the Outlaws and Pac, and Pac was clowning him.

"I was listening to these fools, and laughing in my head because they were funny, and Pac turns to me and says, 'Leslie, man, why you always quiet? Why you ain't got nothin' to say?' I said, 'I'm just listening to y'all.'

"So he goes off on this routine to the Outlaws, that he's Leslie's bodyguard. He works for me, I don't work for him. We get to the club, and there's this beautiful Latin female. She was so beautiful, I can't emphasize it enough. She was waiting for the valet to bring her car, and she turns to look at Tupac. They locked eyes and she said, 'Excuse me, Tupac?' He turned to look at her and he said, 'Yes?'

" 'Can I ask you something?'

"He said, 'Go ahead.' And she said, 'But it's kind of personal.'

"She then motioned with her finger for him to come to her. Tupac walked toward her and she leaned over and whispered in his ear, 'Can I have a kiss?'

"He backs up and looks at her, with a look like, Damn, I don't even know you. And she just smiled at him, she was super sexy and she knew it. He leaned over and gave her a kiss on the cheek and then proceeds to walk back to the club.

"She said, 'Wait a minute, Tupac . . . come here.' He turns again to look at her with a funny look, and walks back in her direction. Again, she leans over and whispers in his ear, 'I mean a kiss on the lips, something to remember you by.'

"He looks at her and slowly leans in to give her a kiss on the lips. They locked lips for a moment, and then he backs away. 'Thank you, Tupac,' she says with a sigh. Now, he turns to again walk toward the club, and I looked at him and said, 'Yo Pac. You're fired.' "

Tupac liked to party as much as the next man, but he liked women better. Pussy was number one. Every party, even if he was the center of attention, he'd take off as soon as a woman came into the picture. He didn't sit around and hang out just to be the star, he'd get his groove on and go about his business. He's just like a dog with a bone, he'd take that bone and go and work it in a corner. You never hear from that dog no more until that bone is eaten up. He comes back out, looking for some more.

The thing about Pac is, if he walked into a building full of women, all of them belonged to him. That's just the way he was. I've seen women who have come to fuck Tupac Shakur. It doesn't matter if they had three or four women in front of them, if he's still ready to go, they'll take fifth. The killer part about is, they weren't just hoochies. They were celebrities. One way or another, he touched a lot of women.

"I wish I could have been invisible over the world and watched how many women cried when they found out that man died," says Leslie. Although Les remembers Pac fondly, he and Pac had a problem when it came to women. Pac felt like Les was more interested in checking out the ladies than watching his back.

"Pac had a love for Frank," recalls Les. "The problems Pac wanted to classify as 'Les and women,' he overrode in Frank's case, because he had a special relationship with Frank. That's just how it goes. If I like this guy more than I liked this other guy, then I'm gonna overlook things in his favor."

I don't know if he overrode anything, I just know I handled myself a bit differently. Women were less likely to approach me. Les was always getting into it with Pac and here's a typical scenario.

They were all at the Roxbury club in West Hollywood one night, sitting in a VIP booth. "I'll be damned if this Persian girl didn't walk up to me and say, 'My name's whatever. What's yours?' " says Les. "I leaned over and said, 'My name's Leslie, but I'm working, sweetheart, and I can't talk to you right now.' She said, 'I see Tupac, so you must be his bodyguard. Wait a minute, I want my friends to meet you.'

"I tried to grab her but she slipped away before I could tell her it wasn't a good idea. I said, 'You know what, Lord, are you trying to get me out of this job?' I'm having my talk with God now. She comes over with her two roommates and Pac is still sitting at the table, and she begins the introductions. She had an Asian roommate and a white roommate and the Asian girl went up to Pac and said, 'Hi, Tupac, can I sit in your lap?'

"Pac grabs his dick, and says, 'Yeah.' So she sits in his lap and a little bit of pressure has been relieved for the minute; however, as soon as the Asian girl gets comfortable, all of a sudden the Persian girl jumps in my lap, because by now, I'm sitting down. The chick is fine, Frank knows I love women, but I'm thinking to myself, What am I going to do about this? I wouldn't mind playin', but I know the job comes first."

I don't mind talking about Pac's sex life, because it was something he lived for. He's probably looking down, now, saying, "Frank, you forgot to tell them about this other bitch over here."

I laugh when I think about other books being written on Tupac, where they want him to be some kind of Malcolm X figure. Tupac was Malcolm triple-X!

I asked one of the strippers who worked on the "How Do U Want It" shoot if she fucked him without a condom.

"We started with a condom, then he put it in again and he didn't have one on."

I said, "You should know better."

She said, "I stopped him as soon as I realized what was up." Still, it could've been too late.

From what I could gather, Tupac was pretty responsible but it only takes one time to fuck up.

I talked to one of my friends the other day and she told me she slept with her neighbor, and when I asked her if she used protection, she told me no.

The whole thing is, when you're getting fucked-up and you're thinking about pussy and you don't have a condom, you say to yourself, *Fuck a condom*. It's wrong, but that's the truth.

One of the groupies who used to hang around Pac came up to me once and said, "I know you're fucking as many women as Tupac is."

I set her straight, and told her, "If I wanted to, I could. But I have a wife and I have a daughter and I plan on seeing grandkids one day. If I wanted to be out here fuckin' everything that Tupac was, that would be my business. I'm not, however."

She said, "Uh-huh . . ."

I said, "Why would I have to lie to you? We don't know each other."

She said, "Nigga, please, I know you're getting just as much pussy as he's getting."

I told her the only woman I had to answer to was my wife, and she hasn't asked me that question because she knows the truth.

I didn't put myself in the situation where women thought I wanted anything from them. Pac liked that about me and bragged about me all the time. If I was busy getting pussy, how could I be doing my job?

If I wanted to indulge myself, I could have. But I'm no fool. I'd heard the stories about the girls getting raped by so-and-so's bodyguard and lemme just tell you something, there wasn't going to be no muthafuckin' mistake and no story about me. I was there to do a job, and I did my job. My job didn't include picking up groupies and fucking all these chicks. If it did, I would've been there for that. Other bodyguards looked for that, and he weeded them out. You have to remember something, the man wanted his life protected. The man wanted his back watched.

This didn't mean I didn't know where to find a party, if one needed to be found. One night, Pac was restless and wanted to hit a club. He and Suge like going to a club called Peanuts on Tuesdays, when "Michelle's Triple X" jumps off—it's primarily a lesbian club that night. That night, he wanted to do something different. We'd spent the day hanging out at the Wilshire house, watching basketball and videos. I asked him if he'd ever gone down to Orange County. He said he didn't know any clubs down there, and I told him I did.

"Let me show you a good time tonight, Pac." I had this strip club in mind, called Fritz II. Before we left, he had his mom cook me a steak dinner, and by then, I was starving and grateful. We ate dinner while watching, *Ace Ventura: When Nature Calls.* Pac couldn't get enough of Jim Carrey, and his impersonations were dead-on.

Before we left, I made a phone call to a buddy of mine who worked at this club, while Pac checked with the Outlaws, to see if they wanted to go along. But they were all smoked out, drunk and full, and weren't leaving the couch. "How y'all muthafuckas expect to get some pussy when y'all don't leave out the house to go find it?" he teased them. Only Fatal was game. Pac took his Jag, and we rolled.

Pac had a wad of cash on him, as usual and we went and got a couple hundred dollars in singles. I knew this one waitress who worked there, she worked out at the same gym as me and used to be a checker at the Price Club in my neighborhood. She made good tips at the strip club, and when I saw her, I flagged her down and told her, "Take real good care of my boy here and I guarantee you, he'll take good care of you." I suggested she check with her manager to see if she could wait on our table exclusively all night.

A couple other girls showed up, one was a stripper and the other a waitress. Pac cruised around in the club, he went upstairs for a lap dance, and he chatted with a few of the girls. At one point, I saw him out there and women had actually flocked around him, like fish to food. I told our waitress she might want to get some of these girls away from him, because it wasn't that kind of party, and she did.

We closed the joint down, and he was still ready to party. I took him to this after-hours spot in O.C. called Sensations, and he lost his mutha-fuckin' mind. He was in a party mood to begin with, and when people realized it was Tupac, the freak was on. He didn't leave the dance floor and I could tell he was having a good time.

One of the women who'd been with us from the strip club, and who Tupac had given $600 in tips to throughout the night, started making some noise. I went to see what was going on, and till this day, I don't know if I believe her or not. She said she'd put her purse down between her feet on the floor, and when the song she was dancing to ended, she went down to get her purse, and it was gone.

The entire time, I was standing right there on the dance floor, keeping people away from Pac, while he was dancing with her and her friend. They were dancing in a small circle and I didn't see anybody snatch a purse. Tupac, of course, felt bad for her and we had the whole joint looking for the purse. He peeled off another $600 from his roll and gave it to her. I was so upset, and never got over it. Time and time again, I got on him about it, and he said to me, "Frank, I make $600 in a minute. The girl probably needed the money."

I told him, "Fuck this bitch, you gave her $600 and I don't know if she's lying or not, but I don't like the fact that she's doing you like this. If she lost it, she should just choke it up and not even take your money. She opened her fuckin' hand and took the money." To me, it seemed like a scam. I felt like he'd been used. I got on him for about three or four days, because I felt bad about it.

We continued dancing anyway, and he wasn't bothered by it, only me. At the end of the night, this bitch looks at me and says, "Can I have my money?" I was holding the next $600, and I was hoping and praying, by some miracle, she was gonna forget about it so I could give it back to Pac.

You know when you've had too much of something and you don't want it anymore? Shit, that wasn't the case with Pac and pussy. The boy could fuck. That's my road dog. That's what he loved doing. He didn't have to chase pussy, pussy came to him. Pussy was running up on him, and he wasn't turning it away.

I can say this, for the year of his life that he had left, he enjoyed himself. He did everything he wanted to do. The good life was his for the moment, and he had fun. He played, he fucked, he made money, he traveled, he smoked weed. He did everything that someone would do if it was the last year of their life, and he was good at all of it.

CHAPTER TWELVE

FAMOUS SEXUAL ENCOUNTERS

    Tupac didn't just deal with hoochies and groupies, but many of his women were famous actresses or performers. I'll say one thing about Pac, he did get around. For the most part, he didn't waste his time on average women—only the finest bitches would do.

Salli Richardson

I came to work one day in June; right where the 10 and the 101 meet in downtown Los Angeles, there's an underpass I'll never forget. It was the shoot's location, we were working under a freeway, and it was completely dirty, filthy. It was the second or third week of shooting, and I thought to myself, *Fuck, I can't park here.* It was so nasty, I didn't want to get my Benz all messed up. It was smelly and hot, and Tupac hadn't gotten there yet. It wasn't exactly the kind of place you'd expect a new romance to blossom, but that's exactly what happened that day.

    I was hanging out with another Wrightway security guard, talking about what a shithole the location was, and when Pac got there, I asked him what was on the agenda for the day and he looked up me slyly, "I think Salli Richardson's coming by."

    "Oh, really?" I said.

    "Yeah, she's fuckin' around with dat nigga Babyface's cousin, or some shit," he said.

    "So, she's got a man?" I asked.

    "Not for long," he laughed.

    "Oh yeah, you just think you're the boss playa that you are," I joked with him.

    "Nigga, I *am*, you better recognize that," he said.

We continued to bullshit for a little while, and the makeup artist, Vonda, knocked on the door.

"So, your girl's supposed to come by today?" she asks.

Damn, everybody knew about this girl coming by. Turns out Vonda had introduced the two of them. Tupac had found out she and Salli were friends and he gave Vonda a letter to give to Salli. It had worked like Federal Express, because it wasn't even two days later.

As the day goes on and I'm kickin' it with one of the homeboys, who says to me, "Frank, you see Salli Richardson over there?" I hadn't met her yet. "She is finer than a muthafucka. Wait till you see her," says the homie.

Sure enough, I saw her talking to the director and then watched her walk over to the trailer with Vonda. He wasn't lying. Salli is a very pretty girl, a complete package. Her hair and skin were the same color of caramel brown, and she had a fine little body.

I decided to play bodyguard. "Hey, you guys can't come in here," I joked to Salli and Vonda. "Unless you introduce me to your friend."

Vonda introduced us, and Salli was totally cool with me. I let them inside and I guess this is the first time Tupac and Salli met each other. I was out there for a while, sitting in one of those fold-up chairs at the bottom of the steps, and it occurred to me Tupac would probably like some privacy right about now. So I walked in the trailer and said, "Hey, Vonda, why don't you keep me company, I'm getting bored out here." The timing was perfect. Tupac had that look of mischief in his eye I knew so well.

Check this out, this was all going down around eleven A.M., but Salli didn't leave the trailer until somewhere around five P.M., so they were really getting into each other.

After she left, I went back in the trailer and this nigga's in there, jumping up and down, putting his hand all over his face, talkin' bout, "Nigga! Can you believe it?! Salli Richardson, the finest fuckin' actress out there. Fine sista! I'm gonna fuckin' hook that up."

I said to him, "Now, Pac, she's the kind of material to be your lady, not just somebody to be fuckin' around with."

He said, "yeah, I know, huh? I should kick it on the real with her."

"She's somebody you could put on your arm and go to an awards ceremony with," I said.

He agreed. Pac was sprung. He told me he was gonna hook up with her later that night, and from that day on, Salli was on the set. It got real hot and heavy between the two of them, and before you knew it, she was driving his green convertible Jaguar and kickin' at his Wilshire house.

Me and Kevin Hackie started making bets. "She's just a fly-by-nighter," he said. "Bet she's not around even a month." I agreed. Knowing Pac, Kevin's estimate was generous. We all gave him the benefit of the doubt, though.

Usually, when Salli was in the trailer, I stayed outside the trailer. Vonda used to pop in occasionally and hang with them, and sometimes I would go inside and find Salli laying on top of Pac, with his shirt off. Salli usually wore something like a halter top, and she was definitely into him.

Vonda started telling me stories about Salli. "That's my girl, she's in a relationship with Ol' Boy . . ." She was referring to the dude who was related to Babyface. "I think he's just too soft for her and she wants a thug, she wants a hard nigga. I think her and Tupac's gonna get a along really good."

From what I gathered from Vonda, Salli was *really* into Pac. She'd never been with anybody like him, and was down for a brotha who was so controversial, and the fact that he was a bad boy, a roughneck.

He must've felt the fever, too, because one day, he called up a Death Row employee named Roy and had him purchase a necklace for her, with a diamond heart locket. Probably cost him somewhere around $15,000—Pac didn't care about the price.

When the package showed up, I brought it into the trailer for her. She and Pac were in bed and I didn't see her response to the gift, but I sure heard it. When she came out of the trailer, she was wearing it, and she winked at me. She was beaming.

The necklace wasn't the only thing making it clear how Pac felt about her. An incident happened that made it very apparent. Leslie had taken a picture with Salli, but then lost the picture. When he wanted to take another one, word got out to Tupac first and he completely snapped. It was a harmless thing, but Leslie made the mistake of bragging about it. But it got worse. Leslie also said something to Salli about not seeing her in any recent movies—he was just wondering if she was still acting or what was up. She told Tupac and it made a bad situation worse. Leslie became Tupac's least-wanted bodyguard He always got a little too close to the women for Tupac's taste. He ended up firing Leslie off the set, and Wrightway came down on him. Turned out Les had snapped the picture for his wife.

But everyone knew you just shouldn't mess with Pac's women, even if you're just making conversation. And Salli was definitely one of his women at this point in time. This was still at the beginning of their affair and he was on that, "This is my woman, this is my bitch" roll, which means all hands off and watch your eyes. It wasn't easy to do with Salli, because she was so pleasant and affectionate. Once she got to know me, she always had a hug or a smile. She was as friendly as can be. Of course, she saved her main affection for Pac, and he was on cloud nine. They were having picnics at his house, they even had a picnic at the Malibu house—a house I never saw because I never got invited to any of the Malibu house parties he threw, and one day he told me why.

"Frank, you'd come over there, take your shirt off, and I'd never get any of the bitches," Pac said. True to form, he never once invited me to that house, and I'm pretty sure he was serious about the reason. It was, after all, right on the beach. But he didn't live there very long because the celebrities of the colony had him evicted. I guess there was one too many noise violations, and it was a very exclusive colony.

He and Salli continued making some noise of their own. She kept showing up every day, following us to different locations, and when she took off one evening, I started messing with him. "You know I got the 411 from Vonda, nigga. What's up, what you gonna do?"

Pac said, "Man, she's fine, she's bad. I'm gonna kick it with her for a while."

I said, "A'ight, just treat her good if you want her around."

No sooner than I said that, the relationship was over.

I was off for two days, and by the time I came back, Salli wasn't around anymore, but this girl who was supposedly his "housekeeper," and was staying with him at his new house in Calabasas, was around.

The first thing I noticed, was the convertible Jaguar was back on the set, but he wasn't driving it. He'd bought himself a white Land Cruiser. I asked him how come he had two cars on the set.

"I took the Jag back from Salli," he said.

"What happened?" I asked.

All he said was, "Fuck that bitch."

End of story.

As quick as it started, it was over. Probably lasted only two weeks total. I tried to get the 411 from Vonda but she didn't know what went down—all she knew was Salli was at home, heartbroken. There was some "he said, she said" bullshit, and Pac cussed Salli out. Apparently, someone had spread a rumor that Pac asked Salli to marry him and that's what started the argument. Whatever Salli did say, had supposedly gotten back to Kidada Jones, who was going out with Pac at the time. Kidada's the daughter of Quincy Jones and Pac was seeing her.

One thing I do know for a fact is he didn't propose to Salli, because he would have said something to me. It wasn't no love in the air, it was fresh sex—it had nothing to do with wedding bells and shit; it was too fast, for him anyway.

I suspect what really happened was Pac started getting that ol' feeling of a woman being around, and he couldn't adapt to it. It wasn't his thing. He wasn't all up on that girlfriend shit, after all.

Madonna

When we were working on *Gridlock'd*, we had a lot of time to shoot the shit because we were sitting around for eight weeks. The funny thing about moviemaking is people think it's all excitement and action, but a lot of the time, you're just waiting around for scenes to be set up or for people to be called to the set.

We had eight weeks to spend together in the trailer, confined. Either we're gonna fight, fuck, or not get along. Since it was me and Pac, obviously we weren't fucking or fighting. We spent the downtime talking about things.

We were watching a talk show, and it was during Madonna's pregnancy, and they flashed a picture of Carlos Leon and Madonna walking into a New York building on the screen. Leon is the father of Madonna's baby girl Lourdes. Pac had just rolled a blunt and after he finished inhaling a big toke, he said, "You know, that used to be me."

I said, "Yeah, right, get the fuck outta here," thinking he was just fuckin' with me.

"Nigga, I'm serious, that was me," he said, and I could tell he was. "Lemme tell you something, anytime I tell you something about a bitch, it's for real."

I said, "A'ight. So what's up between you and ol' girl?"

He said, "Nothing."

I said, "Did you know her, then?"

"Dude," he said, "I used to spend time with Madonna in New York."

I said, "You did?" *Damn,* I'm thinking, *this brotha does get around.*

That was the end of the conversation. He never mentioned her again, and I have no reason to believe he was lying.

Jada Pinkett

Once again, we were watching a movie on the set of *Gridlock'd.* I used to bring movies for us to watch in the trailer. He loved Jim Carrey, he used to imitate that muthafucka all the time—by far, he was Pac's favorite. But we were chilling in the trailer, and we started talking about Janet Jackson and his time on *Poetic Justice.* He said, "I don't like that bitch. She wanted me to take an AIDS test just to kiss her. I was like, Fuck that, if I've got to take one, she's got to take one, too." He really didn't like her. Yeah, she wanted him to take an AIDS test but if you saw the movie, you'll remember the only good thing in it was Tupac. The boy could act his ass off.

Around that time, somebody popped in a copy of *Jason's Lyric,* and during the scene where Jada Pinkett's getting fucked by ol' boy on the counter, I said to Pac, "Damn, she ain't got no ass."

He laughed and said, "That could have been my ass."

I said, "What?!"

"Yeah, way back in the day, she was in a couple of my videos."

I was trippin', looking at this fine bitch and wondering what went down.

"She was too far out there for me," he said.

Jada's with Will Smith right now. Lucky man.

Faith Evans

During the time Tupac was in prison, one of the thoughts that kept him going was the idea that when he got out, he was gonna fuck Faith Evans, the wife of Notorious B.I.G. He told me, straight up: "The first thing I did when I got out of prison was I fucked Faith. Every bitch I say I'm gonna fuck, I fuck em."

Adina Howard

Adina Howard, an R&B singer with a big, big bootie, came a-knockin' on the trailer one day.

Leslie was on duty and he said to me, "You know who that is, right?"

I said, "No. Who?"

"It's Adina Howard, she cut her hair."

It was really short and blonde at the time and I didn't recognize her. She walked into the trailer and I followed her.

"Oh, Pac, I didn't know you had company," I lied, because of course I saw that bootie walking in.

He introduced us and that was that, and I stepped out.

He never mentioned her again so I don't know what kind of relationship they had. But if you look at Pac's history, I wouldn't be surprised if they got busy on some level.

Arnelle Simpson (O. J.'s daughter)

My alternate bodyguard was on duty on this particular Tuesday. This was during the time Tupac was still living in the Peninsula Hotel in Beverly Hills. As soon as I pulled up to valet, Tupac cruised up behind me.

"Big Frank!" he shouted. "Wassup?"

We greeted each other and he said, "Let's chill up in the room."

I said, "Cool." When I turned to look at who he was with, I thought, *Damn, she looks familiar.* I couldn't quite place the face, though.

Kevin walked over to me and said, "You know who that is, right?"

I fessed up, and told him no.

"Arnelle Simpson."

I said, "Get the fuck out of here." This was during the height of the O. J. trial and he may as well have said "Princess Di."

"We just came from the movies, and he was all over her," Kevin said. (Arnelle, who is a video stylist in the music industry, has said elsewhere that her meeting with Tupac that night was purely professional.)

When I showed up, I went to my room and I realized Pac wasn't going out. I wondered what was up, and I called down to his assistant, Kendrick, and asked what was up.

He said, "He's still with Arnelle." I asked if he was going to be doing anything or going out, and he said, "I don't think so."

Time went by, and he never called me to go out. So I just chilled for the rest of the night.

The next morning was when shit popped off. Pac called me and said, "We're ready to roll."

I went down to the lobby with my wife Lori, who always stayed with me when I was working at the Peninsula. Lori took one look and said, "That's Arnelle Simpson!"

We went over to the apartment complex in the Valley where the Outlaws lived, because Arnelle's 900 convertible SAAB was parked there. Why, I have no idea.

After Arnelle left, when we got into the Outlaws' stinky apartment, Pac started bragging to 'em. Everybody started rolling up blunts, and as they're smoking, Pac starts telling them all about Arnelle.

He was so excited. He was jumping up and down. "Arnelle Simpson. The baddest bitch in L.A. right now, the finest sista!!!Big ass!!!Y'all see that ass? Y'all see that ass? That ass was big!!!"

He was so excited and so proud. Everybody started jumping up and down, and high-fivin' and screaming and shit. As I look back on that moment, I remember Tupac's excitement and how he started telling the Outlaws about a video he had in his head. It was gonna be like, "Murder Was the Case," Snoop's 20-minute video, and each of the Outlaws were going to have roles they played in it.

It hurts me so much to think back on that time and see that excited nigga, and remember the dreams he had that weren't fulfilled.

Kidada Jones

Several times when I was leaving Pac, after bringing him to his house or wherever he was staying at the time, Kidada Jones would be walking in as I was walking out. The first time I passed by her, was in an elevator. The door opened right when I was leaving, and she happened to be getting out as I was about to get in. I didn't know who she was, but I greeted her by saying, "Hi, how are you?"

She walked right by me. I was only being polite. I wasn't in her face,

I just offered her a simple greeting. She acted like I was invisible, and just walked right through the door. I'm not an easy man to miss, so I believed it was intentional. I walked in the elevator, and just kept on going, but it stuck with me. Rudeness at this level was something I hadn't encountered much.

The next time I saw her, I asked Pac, "Who is that?"

He said, "Oh, that's Kidada."

I said, "Who's Kidada?"

He said, "Quincy Jones' daughter."

I said, "Oh, she's rude." Just like that, didn't think twice about telling him how I felt.

I spoke with Yaasmyn (a close friend of Tupac's mother whom he treated like an aunt and who ran one of his business enterprises) about her also, and Yaasmyn was very diplomatic. "She's just different, Frank," she said. "We have a hard time with her, too."

Until then, I was taking it personal. I didn't learn until later on she was like that with others. I didn't know what was going on, and I used to wonder, Why is that girl always mean to me? I figured out later she had some serious attitude, and she could take that and keep it somewhere else.

Nevertheless, Pac had his reasons for hanging out with the bitch. He knew Kidada Jones was the daughter of the most established black man in the entertainment industry. He had nothing but respect for Quincy.

I remember walking into work one day—again, this was while we were shooting *Gridlock'd* where a lot of the action took place—and he showed me a cassette collection that he said belonged to Quincy Jones. Tupac said he'd had dinner with Quincy and Kidada the night before at their house, and Quincy loaned the collection to Tupac—it was his entire collection of music he'd produced, from Michael Jackson on down. He had them in a big old satchel, and they were all in order by year, name, and category.

I said, "Pac, what's this?"

He said, "Ah nigga, that's Quincy's shit. I'm getting ready to hook up with Quincy, he's gonna do some shit for me." I asked him what he was talking about, and he said, "Movies, music, you name it, I'm gonna have Quincy produce some shit for me."

I said, "Are you serious?"

I knew he was.

I said, "Nigga, you crazy . . ."

He said, "Frank, Kidada's young, and I'm gonna train her."

I didn't know what to say, so I just nodded.

This wasn't the only time he said some shit about Kidada. When we were in Italy, Michael Moore said to me, "Frank, what do you think Pac sees in Kidada?"

I told him, "I don't have a clue what he sees in her."

You have to know Kidada to understand where we were coming from. Pac was with so many beautiful, classy and cool women. He wasn't only hanging out with women who were just pretty, he had some exceptional women—I'd put Salli in that category.

Kidada didn't have such obvious qualities. She was only nineteen or twenty, and she had short hair. She kept complaining about her hair to her friend Carla, who worked for *Vibe* magazine and accompanied us on the trip.

On our way to the Versace fashion show, she was still moaning about her hair, and Tupac said, "Why don't you take that shit out your hair, then you won't have to complain about it, and I ain't got to hear it no more."

I don't know if she knew he was fucking other women when he was with her. Others knew it, Carla knew it.

After his death, she told people she and Pac were engaged. He never said to me he was gonna get married, or he was thinking about getting married, or that he was engaged to Kidada. The only two people who know for sure are Pac and Kidada.

No matter how I look at it, Kidada left a bad taste in all our mouths. She treated us really bad. I'm sure growing up rich had something to do with it, but, to my mind, there is no excuse for being rude.

His "Wife," Keitha Morris

When you don't have shit, and you're a regular muthafucka off the street, if you get locked down, the first thing you do when you come out of prison is you brag about it. If you're an entertainer, like in the case of Rick James, James Brown, and Tupac, do you think they went around bragging about the time they were locked up in jail? No, they don't. The reason they want to forget about that shit is because they have careers. They have something that made them who they were. Prison didn't give them an identity. They already had one.

They don't talk about it and for the most part, real G's don't either. Anybody else who's been there, already knows what they've been through. So Tupac never discussed his jail time. Except one day, while we were talking in his trailer, somehow it came up that I'd been married three times.

"Damn, Pac," I said. "You ain't never gettin' married."

"I was married," he said.

"You were?"

"Yeah, to a friend of mine. She was real cool, I got married in prison so we could have sex." With that marriage certificate, he was allowed to have conjugal visits. "That's why I got pissed when I'd hear muthafuckas talking about how I got raped in jail," he said, "because I ain't getting raped in no muthafuckin' jail, ain't no one steppin' to me trying to take my muthafuckin' manhood."

The marriage ended right as he was getting out of prison, and he took care of her.

CHAPTER THIRTEEN

ITALY

Right before *Gridlock'd* wrapped, we were sitting in the trailer and he busted out with, "You know we're going to Italy next week."

"For real?"

"Yeah, it's Men's Fashion Week, and you know I'm gonna be there. But check this, I don't think you can carry a gun in Italy so we need to hook up with another bodyguard. We need another big nigga."

I asked him who he liked, and he picked this brotha, Rich, another LAPD officer who moonlights as a security guard. Rich was down, until he found out what he'd be getting paid—the standard $200 a day from Wrightway—and he backed out. For him, it wasn't worth taking the time off work.

I told Pac and he said, "What!!! Not enough money! He's turning down Italy, talkin' about not enough money. Shit, getting paid's the bonus."

We wound up with Michael Moore, the member of the security team who is also a fire captain. Pac was satisfied. He liked the idea of showing up in Milan with two of Cali's biggest, blackest brothers. It made him look good.

The entire trip was being set up through Quincy Jones' office, who was handling it for *Vibe* magazine. One of Kidada's best friends, Carla, worked in public relations for *Vibe*, which is partially owned by Quincy, and they hooked it all up for Pac.

Yaasmyn sent me a schedule on June 25, and we wrapped *Gridlock'd* on the twenty-sixth. I looked it over and couldn't believe how crazy we were gonna be. In just a couple of days, Pac was going to twelve fashion shows, as well as after-parties. It was insane. When Pac scanned it over, the first thing he noticed was me and Michael weren't allowed into the

Dolce and Gabbana show. He and Kidada were confirmed to be front-row guests but because of space, we were supposed to wait outside. Tupac said, Fuck that. If we weren't going in, he wasn't going in. So true to his word, that was the one show we didn't go to. We all had front-row seats at every other show that week.

Before we made it to Italy, however, we had to meet with Kidada in New York at the airport. This was the first time I was going to officially meet her, and it was as unpleasant for me as I suspected it would be. We were all up in a VIP area, and Pac introduced us to her as his bodyguards and she barely moved her head. It was the most nonchalant greeting I've ever had, just cold as ice.

We got on the plane and it was one long-ass flight. Pac and Kidada flew first-class and we were riding coach. We finally landed in Milan on June 29 at eight-thirty A.M., and as soon as we checked into our rooms at the Hotel Principe di Savoia—a five-star hotel—we had to turn around and get Pac to his first fitting, which was at Versace's boutique. Keep in mind, we'd been on a plane since June 28, our chaperons, Michael and Jeff, gave us thirty minutes to get downstairs to make it in time for the fitting and we didn't even get the chance to change our clothes from the airplane ride, so me and Michael were still wearing shorts.

The first thing Tupac wanted was pot. Someone was supposed to have hooked up some weed for Pac as soon as he arrived.

"Find some!" said Pac. "I thought it was already set up."

"We're working on it," Pac was promised.

"Damn, I need some weed," said Pac.

We were sitting in Carla's room, and we got up to leave, and Pac was fuming. "I'm gonna go fuckin' crazy if we don't find any weed," he said. "Can't be without pot for a week!"

He was bitchin' to us throughout the whole trip. "If I'd a known we weren't gonna get stopped in customs, I could have brought my own weed!" At this point, he's losing his mind.

"What are we gonna do, I can't just be straight like this," he said.

He ended up spending a potless week, but all he could talk about was Amsterdam. How far is it, and can we drive there? Someone told Pac you could order pot off a menu at restaurants in Amsterdam, and he was like, *Fuck Italy, get me to Amsterdam.*

* * *

Tupac had a sound check directly after the Versace fitting, because he was going to be performing that night, and then we walked him to his next fitting, this time it was for Valentino. He did a couple of interviews in between and by that time, it was nine P.M. and we were off to Versace's fashion show."

Now, I'm a black man who grew up in the projects, I had no fuckin' idea who Gianni Versace was. The fact that I got to meet him and his family when I'm from that side of the tracks is pretty amazing. When we first met him, we met him at his store, and they'd been expecting us. They assigned us a chaperon, and rolled out the red carpet for us.

I noticed that his sister, Donatella and her daughter had more security than Tupac, and I asked one of the Italian guards what was up. He said the family couldn't go anywhere without an entourage of bodyguards because Gianni's life had been threatened. I learned the little girl was the biggest target, and they'd already made preparations in case something were to happen. They expected if she got kidnapped, she would be taken to Naples or Rome, where the majority of Italy's crimes occur, and more than likely she'd be held hostage underground. It gave me an eerie feeling because they seemed like such kind people and the girl was so young. For his part, Gianni was a genuinely nice person, who I could tell was very loved by the people around him.

After Pac's rehearsal of the song he was gonna perform, "California Love," we went to another room of the house and had dinner, and Gianni came in; everyone stood up. He walked to our table, and gave each of us a kiss and a hug. He gave Pac one of those European kisses, he went along about it, but I could tell he wasn't thrilled with it. I was quick to stick my hand out, because I don't play that shit. Not even with Versace.

I look back now, and realize what a special opportunity it was to meet him, though. I want to send my condolences to his family. They were so cool with us, and I'm sorry they lost someone so special to them.

We got back to the hotel. Earlier in the night, Kidada told Pac she'd be in the room when he got back or she would leave the key at the front desk so he could get back in his room. There was only one key to the rooms in this hotel, and if you lost it, you'd have to get an escort from the hotel to open it for you. They wouldn't issue two keys.

He asked her, "You definitely gonna be here when I get back?"

She said she would, but that she might get something to eat with Carla. If she did, she'd leave the key.

When we got back, the key wasn't at the front desk. So we went upstairs, and no one comes to the door. He started kicking the door, and I said, "Pac, that ain't gonna do no good. If nobody's in there, nobody's in there."

"Fuckin' bitch," he yelled. "I'm gonna kick her fuckin' ass."

I tried to calm him down, and said, "Don't even talk like that. It'll be cool. We're over here in Italy, let's just chill . . ." For the record, he never hit Kidada. I never saw him hurt her and any signs that he hurt her. But boy, was he pissed.

He turned around and took off walking, real fast. We got down to Carla's room and she wasn't there, either. We went back down to the lobby and asked the concierge to let us in.

We get back to the room and notice the key is now in the door.

He enters the room, sees Kidada and starts yelling at her. He turned to me, and said, "Frank, we ain't going nowhere. If we do, I'll call you."

So I went back to my room with Michael.

Sure enough, Pac calls me and says, "Let's get the fuck out of here."

We went to a trendy Milan club called Club Hollywood, and it was packed—people were dropping shit all over the floor, dancing and going all crazy. When they recognized who he was, everybody just freaked the fuck out. Pac jumped in the deejay booth, and did an impromptu performance of "How Do U Want It." Needless to say, he's a huge superstar in Europe and he had his pick of the ladies. Ironically, he met up with a girl he knew from Cali, the ex-wife of a rocker. She was petite, about five foot five inches tall, and she was wearing this powder-blue spaghetti-strap short dress. It was really sheer, and you could see the T-back of her white panties. She was really sexy—the bitch was fine.

We went back to the hotel, because it turned out she was staying at the same place as we were, and Pac tells me, he's gonna be in ol' girl's room tonight.

The next morning, I saw him and asked what happened.

He said, "Shit, I fucked ol' girl all night, and then I went down to my room and fucked Kidada."

I said, "Get outta here!"

He said, "I got back to my room, and Kidada was all over me."

I was like, "Wha?"

Me and Michael started cracking up.

I said, "How'd you do it, Pac?"

He said, "I'm exhausted, but I pulled it off. I fucked the shit out of her, too."

This was just the beginning of his sexual exploits in Italy.

Italy in June is piping hot. We were being shuttled around in this heat from fitting to fitting, show to show, and it was crazy.

Tupac was enjoying all the clothes they were giving him. He was laughing about a nigga getting hooked up with thousand-dollar pants and thousand-dollar shirts. He loved it, though, because all he had to do was show up at the shows looking fresh. We went to Gianfranco Ferre's fashion show at eleven-thirty A.M. on June 30, and he wore some of his Versace gear. He had on these black leather pants with a moiré pattern, and it came with a matching vest and get this, matching boots. He wasn't wearing a shirt underneath, and he was stylin'. Versace loved Tupac, and gave him so much gear it was crazy. He was loving it.

At most of the shows, you'd run into the same people. We started seeing familiar faces, and these two women stood out in particular. They were Italian ladies. One looked like she was in her mid-thirties, and on this particular day, she was dressed in yellow from head to toe. She was wearing yellow pants, a yellow jacket, and yellow pumps. She had hazel eyes and long dark hair and I noticed her because she stood out. Tupac noticed her as well.

Michael and I were sitting on one side of the runway, and Tupac and Kidada were on the other side. This lady was on the same side as me and Michael, and at one point, we watched her get up and walk over to the other side near where Tupac was sitting. She started talking to a friend of hers and her friend was drop-dead gorgeous. She was breathtaking. All this was happening while the fashion show was going on, and before I knew it, it was over and it was time to head over to the Romeo Gigli fitting.

It was about three-thirty in the afternoon, and it was still hot as fuck.

By now, I'm hot, tired, and needed to sit down for a minute. The schedule had us going for 24-7 and while Tupac was being fitted, I found a chair and sat down for a minute. Michael Moore came over and sat with me. I could see the designer eyeing Michael Moore and me, it was very obvious. Tupac was going to be in this fashion show so the fitting was taking awhile. Kidada was also trying clothes on.

Romeo Gigli motioned over to Michael, and I watched the two of them talk for a moment.

Tupac eventually ended up in the conversation, and Michael started walking over to me.

"They want us in the show," he said.

"I'm not getting in that show," I said. "That shit's going to end up in magazines, people will be taking pictures. Suge's gonna flip his lid."

From the get-go, we were told not to take pictures with artists, and to stay far away from acting like groupies. We were to maintain professional standards all the time. The issue kept coming up in meetings a lot though, because Leslie and Pac had their run-ins.

I said no, and told Michael he could do whatever he wanted. I'd already had a little incident with Pac, that made me think it wasn't such a good idea. Some dude at one of the shows kept asking me who I was, with Pac standing right there. He asked my name and I told him.

"Frank Alexander, hmmm . . . Do you compete in bodybuilding contests?"

I nodded. He then asked if I was a pro, and I nodded again.

"Did you compete in Mr. Olympia?"

I just shook my head, because I was trying to shine the guy on but he was persistent.

"What do you compete in?"

Before I could say anything, Tupac jumped in and said, "Goddamn, man, he said he don't fuckin' know you." Then he looked at me and said: "Can you keep your fuckin' groupies out of your face?"

He was totally serious, and I just laughed. Michael Moore started laughing at me, because he could see what was going on.

Nevertheless, here we are with Romeo Gigli trying to get us to share the limelight, and I politely decline.

Tupac walked over to me, and said, "What's up, Frank? You don't want to be in the fashion show? Bullshit! If I got to be in it, you've got to be in it."

I said, "Pac, come on, man . . . I can't be doing that."

He said, "Everybody's in it, and that's that."

The designer called me over, to begin our fitting.

I whispered to Michael, "You have no idea the shit we're going to be in because of this."

He whispered back, "We may as well get our fifteen minutes of fame— who knows what could come from it?"

They didn't have an easy time figuring out what to put us in. Romeo Gigli's clothes weren't exactly designed for bodybuilders.

All they could find was a pair of brightly colored, striped short-sleeved shirts that fit us glove-tight. They had no pants, so we wore our own black shorts. He also made shoes, so he found us a couple pair of sandals.

We went to Gianni Versace's castle after we left the fitting, for his fashion show. We were backstage at the castle, Naomi Campbell was at the show, and I remember when I first saw her backstage.

"Pac, check it out, there's Naomi Campbell," I said.

"*Shut up, nigga, I see her,*" he said.

He didn't want it to look obvious that he was checking her out.

But there were so many women, it was crazy, and it just continued getting crazier.

The next stop was the Byblos fashion show, and sure enough, we see the lady in yellow again, and she was with her beautiful friend. Pac was checking her out, and he eyeballed me to look in her direction, and I saw what was going on.

I knew it was only a matter of time before Pac made his move.

He couldn't say to either of us, "Can you get her number or see what's up?" Not with Kidada around. It was more like, *Shit, nigga, look at that* . . . He was plotting.

The next fashion show on our itinerary was the Dolce and Gabbana show, but Tupac didn't want to go because he was pissed at the designer for not allowing us to attend. He didn't want to be without us not because he was scared, but because he liked the image. The next fashion show was two hours later, at around eight-thirty P.M., and it was for the Valentino show. He'd already been fitted for the show, and was wearing a brown pinstripe suit with white shoes and it was so fuckin' sharp. It was gangsta style, old school, and he looked real good.

Tupac had never been invited to anything like this before and he loved the combination of music and fashion. All the shows had loud music pumpin' out and everybody was festive.

On July 1, it was more of the same, fashion shows, fittings, interviews. It was crazy. The next day was the day of the Romeo Gigli show. The entire fashion show was a trip. Everything was all seventies psychedelic shit, really bright colors and crazy patterns.

Sure enough, flashbulbs were going off everywhere. I wasn't nervous, I'd walked down enough catwalks in my days as a bodybuilder, in front of thousands of people, and I didn't have stage fright.

People were running around us, and it was chaotic. There must've been about two or three hundred people backstage. I met Tyson, the bald black supermodel, and saw so many beautiful women, it was mind-blowing. Everybody was changing clothes in front of everybody else, walking around butt-ass naked, nobody cared if anybody was looking.

I was pretty impressed with that, because it showed the professionalism that came with modeling. It wasn't like people were trying to stare at somebody's pussy or dick, or anything like that. Except of course, for Tupac. I have pictures of him doing it, too.

At one point, Michael, me, and one of the models in the show were talking to Tupac. This one particular model was a white guy, and he actually came over to where we were standing and pointed out this one chick who was changing her clothes.

She was standing behind a rack of clothes, but the clothes were spread apart so you could what she was doing, and she had it going on. She had body. She had *b-o-d-y*.

Our back was to her before this guy came up to talk to us, but we all turned around and looked after he pointed her out. At one point, she bent down and started slowly putting on her stockings, and she had nothing on—not a stitch of clothing—all we could see was her ass and her pussy, and her hands moving up her legs as she pulled her stockings up.

Pac squeaked out, "Oh my God . . ."

All of our mouths were probably on the floor.

There's no doubt about it, Pac was ready to move. He loved Italy. "This shit is cool," he said. "I could do this all day long." Every other show, we were in front, but this time, we were behind the curtain, and it was a whole different view.

You couldn't help but notice how beautiful the women were in Italy. Not just the supermodels, but the Italian women. Pac loved them, and the one thing he kept pointing out was their eyes—he loved Italian women's eyes. There was just something about them. I knew exactly what he was talking about. Eyes on women in Italy were unlike any you find in America. They came in colors I'd never seen before, and combined with their skin tone, so many of them were drop-dead gorgeous.

Tupac was ready to party, and he was getting ready to get free.

We take a town car back to the hotel, Tupac and Kidada are in the back of the car, and I'm in the front with the driver. We could hear them arguing in the back, and me and the driver looked at each other. I started to laugh, silently.

He said to her, "Woman, I am fuckin' tired of doing everything y'all want me to do. I've done everything on the schedule to the letter, and when do I get to have my fun? I ain't got no fuckin' weed, I can't go out and get drunk. We've got two nights left here, and I'm going out with my home-boys."

He was referring to me and Michael. We'd been elevated to homeboy status.

"We're gonna go out and have some fuckin' fun I ain't doing shit no more."

First thing everybody started doing was coming up to me and saying, "Frank, go talk to Pac."

I said, "Fuck that! You just heard the man. He just told all y'all he don't want nothing to do with y'all."

What sense did it make for me to go talk to him when he was all upset? I knew what was going on. He wanted to *pah-tay* and he picked the right night. It was the Dolce and Gabbana after-party and it was slammin'. He asked Carla if she wanted to join us, and she said, "Is Kidada going?"

Pac said, "No."

So Carla said it wouldn't be right if she came along.

He said, "Yeah, I understand that. She's your homegirl, so you go ahead and stay with her, but me and my homeboys are going to go out and have fun."

Pac turned to me and said, "Do not plan on sleeping. We haven't done anything since we've been here and we're gonna be staying up for the rest of this trip."

I looked at him like he was crazy. We had forty-eight hours left in Italy, and I was saving some of that time for the bed.

Someone in the camp took the hint, and scored Pac some Ecstasy. They had fourteen tabs, and they gave everybody going out two apiece.

We go to the party and it's set up like a big rave, with deejays and a bumpin' sound system. There's a zillion people, and it's hot and sweaty. Everybody's getting it on, and lo and behold, guess who's there? The girl we've been seeing everywhere, and she's with her beautiful friend and some dude.

Pac made a beeline exit in her direction, and that's all she fuckin' wrote. She came toward him and he pulled her out onto the dance floor. They were bumpin' hip-hop, and I don't know if the deejay spotted Pac or not, but somebody put on "California Love" when they hit on the floor. Tupac was already on Ecstasy and was getting his drunk on, and when he heard the music, he got buck-wild. Pac dances real nasty, grinding, grabbing tits, grabbing ass—it was like fuckin' with your clothes on. He grabbed her by the waist, and he's got his leg between hers, and they were grinding up and down and she's going with the flow. He's decided in his head already, *I'm fuckin' this bitch.* She was being receptive to him, and they continued to dance all night long.

He came up to me, and asked me for another hit of X. He knew I wasn't taking mine and he wanted to know where the other ones were.

He got back out on the dance floor and hooked up with the chick again, and this time she brings her friend. She introduces Pac to the girl and the three of them start dancing. I cannot even begin to describe how fine this girl was. I've never said this about anyone before, but this girl was a "10." A ten. Gorgeous, gorgeous, gorgeous, gorgeous girl.

I'm looking at Pac like a scientific experiment now. He's on the dance floor getting it on with both these chicks now!

He comes running over to me again. "Frank, do you see those bitches

I'm with?!" he said. "Goddamn, they're fine. But Frankie, I'm fucked up. I'm *fucked up.*"

"Don't worry, Pac," I said. "I've got your back. I've got your back."

He went back out on the dance floor, and the women were all over him.

Me and Michael are trippin'. "What the fuck man?" I said. "He's gonna fuck both these bitches, I bet you."

It's somewhere about three A.M., and we've been at this party since ten.

Our feet are starting to hurt and our eyes are all red from the smoke, but Pac's like the Energizer Bunny out there, he's still going and going, and X is giving him the juice to keep it up. He's on fire. At some point in the night, he offered the women some Ecstasy also, so they could keep up with him.

The party starts dying down at four A.M., and as we're walking out to leave, Pac puts his arms around both the girls and they start following him to his car. I get in the car with them, and Michael Moore drives with one of the chaperons.

I slip into the front seat with the driver, and Pac and the two women sit in the back. As soon as they settle into the car, the driver and I simultaneously pull our visors down. We look at each other and grinned. They both have mirrors.

I wasn't gonna miss this party.

Not a word was spoken from the back, all you could hear was the smooching sound of kisses, sucking noises, and moaning. I watched as Pac kissed the first girl, we'll call her "Yellow," and I could see his hand slip up under the dress of "Ten." Ten starts moaning and I watch her lean back and push her pussy harder toward his hand. He still hadn't stopped kissing Yellow, and she had her lips wrapped around his mouth, and they were darting tongues back and forth.

He turns away from Yellow, and begins kissing Ten, with his hand still under her dress. Suddenly, Yellow's head disappears out of view and now Tupac's moaning.

I'm looking in the rearview mirror, watching it all, thinking, *Oh my God.* I'm only human, and this was some of the horniest shit I'd ever seen.

Me and the driver are trippin' now, we're snickering and shaking our heads. *Ain't no fuckin' way this night's gonna end without him fuckin' both these bitches,* I think to myself.

It was a long drive back to the hotel, and the three of them were all over each other the entire ride, kissing and fingering and who knows what else.

We make it back to the hotel, and by now it's about five A.M. Michael's at the hotel waiting for us, and all I'm thinking about is sleep. We've got two twin, itty-bitty beds waiting for us—we were way bigger than the beds—and we'd never be so happy to see them.

The car's still out in front of the hotel, and it becomes pretty clear one of the women isn't getting out of the car. It's Ten, and Yellow's trying to convince her to come with them, but she won't leave the backseat. Tupac and Yellow are putting up a good fight, trying to convince Ten she's got to come join the party but Ten isn't budging. So finally Pac tells the driver to take her wherever she wants to go, and we all walk to the elevators to go to our rooms.

Not so fast, says a front desk clerk. He motions Yellow to come over to the desk. He starts talking to her in Italian, and she speaks back. He turns to Tupac, and in English says, "She can't come up with you. She's a whore."

Tupac says, "A whore? She's not a prostitute, dude, I met her at the fashion show."

She begins explaining to the guy who she is and what she does, in Italian, and they still won't let her in.

Another guy comes over and asks her for identification, and she hands it over. He then has her fill out a form. Then he makes a phone call. I couldn't believe this shit. If they worked like this in Beverly Hills, the hotels wouldn't have any business.

I have no idea who you call at five A.M. in Italy to check out if a woman's a prostitute. I don't know if he called the police or ran her name through some whore security checklist, but he finally relented.

We walk over to the elevator, and suddenly it dawns on me, Where's Tupac taking this woman? He's surely not taking her to his room, because Kidada's gonna be in there.

The only other room is mine and Michael's.

Sure enough, Pac turns to me and says: "Frank, you know I got to go to your room."

"I figured that."

We get to the room, I let him in, and Michael says to me, "What are we supposed to do?"

"I guess we're out here on the floor," I say.

"Get the fuck out of here," he says. "You got to be kidding me."

Unfortunately, I wasn't.

Michael and I sit our asses down on the floor, we're so tired we don't even care anymore. Suddenly, we both start thinking, *I wonder which bed he's in.*

It was a 50-50 chance.

We're sitting by the door, and we're listening. He's fucking her and we have our ears to the door. What else are we gonna do? It's five o'clock in the morning.

My ear's at one crack and Michael's ear was at the other. The noises coming out of the room were crazy. First, the bed starts squeaking. Then we hear the moaning. Next comes the screaming. It sounds like he's killing the bitch.

Finally, about forty-five minutes later, complete silence.

We're still sitting there, and by now, we're mad as fuck.

Tupac's my boy, though, so I had to say fuck it. He's getting his groove on, nothing I could do.

All of a sudden, the door opens, and both of them tumble out of there. Pac asks me to walk him down to the lobby, so he could get his "date" a car to take her home.

We went back upstairs and Pac went to his hotel room to start packing, and me and Michael returned to our room.

You can imagine how bad our hotel room stank. Guess whose bed was the lucky winner? Mine. The shit was all over the bed, cum and everything, and the room smelled like sex and musk.

Needless to say, I didn't try to catch a catnap. We just got our shit together and got out of there.

It's now July 3, and a car came to pick all of us up, to take us to the Giorgio Armani show in Florence.

We had a couple of hours to kill and Michael and I spent it sleeping in our new room at the Hotel Stazione Leopolda, while Pac spent it with Kidada.

With little to no sleep, we all pile into another car to go to the Armani fashion show.

We'd seen a lot of amazing things that week, but nothing compared to Armani's show. I've never seen anything like it, and I'll probably never have the opportunity to see something as impressive as it again. It was awesome, totally off the hook. I'm sure my jaw dropped a time or two.

The clothes were outrageously hot. The stage was set up like a beach scene, with sand and a blue backdrop with clouds. As one part of the show ended, you'd move into another room with a whole different setup. It went from beach clothes, to spring wear, to office wear, and evening gowns, and each scene was incredible.

As we left, we met Armani and his whole family, and they were all so cool to us.

Who else should we stumble upon but Tupac's old friends, Yellow and Ten, who also happened to be at the show. Kidada wasn't with him, she was still somewhere inside the place. Yellow and Pac gave each other a little more than a wink and a nod, and that was that.

Later that night at dinner, we ate at a restaurant called Vice, and everyone from the trip was there, as well as people we'd run into at the Armani fashion show.

Carla and Kidada were back at the hotel, they were supposed to be packing up to leave the next day, and Pac, of course, had invited his lady friends to hook up with us at Vice. Pac bought everyone in the area where we were sitting drinks, even people he didn't know, he was in such a good mood, and we were all winding down, just having fun.

Pac got up from the table and went to the table behind us, a big-time Italian actress was sitting at the table, as well as this hot-looking blonde buyer from New York. He'd noticed her earlier in the week, and he figured he'd get to know her better. One of the women at the table pointed to me and Michael and asked Pac to explain who we were. He told her, and she asked him why he needed to walk around with bodyguards.

Michael and I turned to listen, wanting to hear what he was going to tell her.

Pac saw us turn around and he said to the woman: "See, that's why I have bodyguards, they heard you talkin' and they automatically turned around like two pit bulls," he said.

Everyone laughed, and it was clear Pac was in the mood to be nice to these people. He was returning some of that Italian love he'd been showered with on his trip to Italy. He wasn't up to anything, he was just cooling out.

After we finished dinner, we went outside onto the street and Pac was still in the mood to party. It was about two A.M., and everything in Florence was pretty much shut down. Someone suggested we go to the Hotel Excelsior, and Pac was still in his "no sleep till Cali" mode, so we went.

It was night two with no sleep, and we were scheduled to leave Italy at seven-thirty A.M.

Pac already had other things in mind. Yellow and Ten were long since gone, and he's working on blonde buyer from New York now. Once again, she's drop-dead gorgeous, and he's worming his way in. We're all hanging out in the lounge area, and they're all drinking and partying. The hotel kept the bar open for us, and we're all having fun. Tupac's acting the fool, and they're all loving it.

Pac turned to me at one point and said, "Frank, let's walk to the bathroom."

We get inside and Pac goes off. "Did you see Blondie? That chick's so fine, that's gonna be my new shit."

"Come on," I said. "Dude, where you gonna fuck her?"

"Her room," he said. "She's staying at this hotel."

"Oh really," I said. "Is that why we came to this hotel?"

"Nah," he said. "All I know, is this is where I'm gonna fuck her."

We laughed and he said, "Nigga, did you see the props you was getting?"

I looked at him, like, *What the fuck* . . .

"Everybody, everybody—all they been talking about is the bodyguards," he says.

"What are you talking about?" I asked. I seriously didn't know what he was saying.

"Everywhere we go, everybody just wants to know about the bodyguards," he said. I still was confused.

"From the fashion show, nigga. Ever since you been in the fashion show, all of Italy's talking about the bodyguards. Every time we go somewhere, every time I hear anything, they talking about you."

I guess everybody noticed us. Wasn't no play coming our way, but shit, it was cool. I figured now was as good a time to tell him thanks for taking me to Italy with him.

"Ah Frankie, you know you're my boy," he said. "You go everywhere I go."

We're both in the stall, still pissing, and feeling good about the trip. He gets back to the mission at hand, telling me what he's gonna do to this girl, and we go back to the lounge. Pac's still clowning, entertaining everybody.

Suddenly I notice this dude picks up one of the huge lounge chairs we're all sitting on and brings it right next to me. He's a designer who works for an Italian design firm based in New York, and it becomes clear he's trying to pick up on me.

This muthafucka was working on me all night long. Figures, the only play I get is from a homosexual male. I didn't care, I was married and I wasn't supposed to be getting any play, but it was still funny. The designer was a good-looking guy, not tall, but handsome. He'd been at the Gigli show and liked what he saw. Michael Moore was trippin' out because he's watching this guy come on to me like he was working a bitch.

"I ain't down for this shit," I whispered to Michael. "I better tell this muthafucka I'm straight."

There were about four or five gay guys with us and the designer was getting aggressive. He was asking me all about me. He wasn't being rude, just persistent. He starts looking at me real intently, and you got to remember, just about everybody was drunk and he was no exception. He even tried to get me to drink mixed drinks by buying me a strong drink. I just put it down in front of me. I'd already had a couple of beers and wasn't planning to drink anymore.

"Frankie, drink, drink," he said. He kept calling me Frankie and started making suggestive remarks. "Yeah, I wanna get Frankie up to my room, that's what I want . . ."

He started asking about my wife, and it began getting a little too personal. He started crossing the line, asking me about sexual preferences, and he asked me to stay a couple of days. It was getting out of hand. He

Left: Tupac on the set of the "I Ain't Mad at Cha" video.

Below: Tupac in heaven, with a Redd Foxx lookalike, in the "I Ain't Mad at Cha" video.

Tupac playing with Heather Hunter on the set of the "How Do U Want It," video, while Frank and director Ron Hightower enjoy the view.

Tupac on the set of the "How Do U Want It" video, with Heather Hunter and Nina Hartley.

Right: Tupac and Frank leaving the trailer for a scene on the *Gridlock'd* set.

Left: Tupac on the set of *Gridlock'd* with Frank's niece, Lemika Early; her wish is granted.

Right: Donatella Versace with Tupac and Kidada Jones backstage at Gianni Versace's mansion.

Left: Tupac performing at the Third Annual Mother's Day Luncheon.

Below: Tupac and his mom at the Third Annual Mother's Day Luncheon.

Right: Frank and Tupac with his family and friends at the Third Annual Mother's Day Luncheon.

Standing: Frank, Leslie, David Kenner, and Suge Knight, with Tupac, flashing the West Coast "W," at the Mother's Day Luncheon.

Frank, Tupac, and Michael Moore in Milan, Italy, fitted to model in the Romeo Gigli fashion show.

Mike Tyson and Tupac in Las Vegas at Suge Knight's Club 662 after the Frank Bruno fight.

Frank and Tupac discussing the next scene for the "How Do U Want It" video with director Ron Hightower.

The bodyguards (left to right): Marcus, Les, Mike, Kenny, Rich, and Frank, after the 1996 Soul Train Music Awards at Monty's in Westwood, California.

Tupac and his Outlaws on the set of the "Hit 'Em Up" video shoot. Bottom row: Kay and Yak Fula (who was murdered shortly after Tupac's death); top row: Muta, Tupac, Malcolm, and Fatal.

Snoop and Tupac on the set of the "Two of Americaz Most Wanted" video.

handed me his business card, with his home phone number, telling me if there's anything I need or I want, to give him a call.

Michael's whispering to me, "Do it, do it, do it." I turn to look at him like he's fuckin' crazy. Michael's just thinking about the free gear I could be getting.

"I'm not saying to do something you don't want to do," Michael said. "Just be nice to the guy."

I realized what Michael was saying now, but fuck it, I'm wasn't gonna lead the guy on. Nevertheless, this went on for hours.

While I was keeping the designer at bay, Pac was trying everything in his power to get Blondie to back to our hotel with him. She was fucked-up, but she wasn't that fucked-up, and he failed.

We went back alone, and luckily, it was within walking distance, but guess who turns up at the Leopolda when we get there? Yellow and Ten. Swear to God. Guess how they knew where to find us. Michael Moore. He'd given them the address.

We walked into the Leopolda and all the lights were off. The two women were on a couch, and Pac starts chatting with Yellow, while Michael Moore is hanging out with Ten. Once again, Pac takes my keys and makes his exit.

Ten wouldn't get on the elevator, she preferred to kick it with us downstairs.

About fifteen minutes later, Pac and Yellow return, and there's about a hour left before we have to leave. We all say good-bye to each other, Michael and I go upstairs and grab our shit out of the room while Pac heads to his room.

Pac gets to his room and finds his shit all over the place. I hear him yelling before I even get to his room

"Fuckin' bitch, didn't pack anything!" Shit, Pac's fuming, and our flight is leaving in forty-five minutes.

Imagine this: Pac had anywhere from $30,000 to $40,000 worth of clothes—shoes, suits, pants, shirts, from every designer in Italy—all spread out.

Me and Michael got to work. We started shoving the clothes in their bags, and luckily, we had some spare bag space, by the time we got done, the shit was loaded. It was so crazy.

We manage to get everything packed, and the cars are still waiting downstairs. We're about twenty minutes from the airport.

"C'mon Pac, we gotta go," I said. "I don't want to miss this flight and I know you don't want to."

"Yeah, no shit," he said.

I told him not to worry about, just to get in the car.

We got to the airport with five minutes to spare, and sure enough, there's a long-ass line when we get there. An official waved us through and started going through our luggage, which was being shipped to Paris, where our connecting flight was supposed to be.

We finally get on the plane, and we were on there just long enough to stress out about missing our connecting flight. As soon as we touch down, they put us on a shuttle to make our connector, and I could swear they were driving us to a completely different airport, it took so damn long.

I run to the ticket counter with everybody's passports and the attendant tells me our flight's already boarded. "You were supposed to have been here an hour ago," she said.

Pac comes over and asks what's up. I told him I was handling it, and he completely loses it again. I calm him down, send him back to where Kidada's sitting, and tell him I'll get us on there. Finally, the attendant makes a call, and we get the green light to start boarding, right before the plane begins taxiing down the runway.

Everyone's on board now, and right as I'm about to take my turn, I get stopped. The attendant fucked up my ticket when she stamped it, and they won't let me on.

The plane is literally pulling away from the gate, and I'm about ready to kill someone. They start taking me seriously and another guy flags down the attendant who stamped my ticket.

Again the plane is stopped and I finally get to board. Except now there's no seats left anywhere. I spend the entire flight, from Paris to Los Angeles, stuck in a middle seat, big-ass, 250-pound Frank, sitting between a French family. I wasn't happy.

Get this—we eventually land in L.A., go to pick up our luggage, and it's lost. Every single one of the bags are gone.

They turned up about a week later, but that wasn't the worst of it. I had to go pick up my bags at Kidada's house, and do you know she didn't call me to tell me my stuff was at her house? I'd given her my phone

number and all my information, but never heard from her. I had to call
the airport to learn my stuff had already been delivered. I called her house,
and the security guard at the gate told me the bags had arrived days ago.
I asked if Kidada knew about it. He said, "Yeah, would you like to
speak with her?"

I said, "No. I don't want to speak to her."

All of my shit was sitting at her house and she didn't have the courtesy
to call me up and tell me about it.

We may have been out of Italy, but our trip wasn't over. About three hours
after we left the airport, Tupac was supposed to perform at the House of
Blues. It was the Fourth of July and when Reggie got word we were back
in L.A., sure enough, he paged us with the word we were working that
night. With all our shit lost, we had nothing to change into and Reggie
ordered us to go all the way home to change. Both of us had on Death Row
T-shirts and shorts, and we'd been in those clothes since the morning
before. We both said fuck it. We're not changing.

We worked outside at the House of Blues for hours, while Death Row
was performing, and the drama wasn't over yet. We had a major incident
that night. One of Tupac's homies, Whosane Fatal, was trying to get inside
and he had a Glock on him. The House of Blues security is also made up
of off-duty officers, and when he tried to go in he got searched and they
immediately took the gun. Pac asked me to intervene, but it was out of my
hands and out of Reggie's hands.

I'd worked with one of the House of Blues brothas before, and he told
me I didn't want to get involved. He broke it down, "Look, why don'cha
all just leave. We need handle this. You don't know the history of this
gun. Someone could have shot fifty people with it." They were planning to
run a ballistics test. Anybody who understands ballistics, knows they can
shoot your gun and tell if it was linked to a murder.

Pac started coming over and I told him, "Go inside, you've got a concert. I don't even want your head filled with this."

"Okay Frank, you go handle it."

The best I could do was get Fatal out of the bullshit. The gun was
taken and he was put in a limo and couldn't come out till the end of the
night. They didn't arrest him and later on the gun was given back to Reggie.
I reported this back to Pac.

"Man, you save us again."

(Later after that, Fatal totaled Pac's brand-new Land Cruiser, and Pac was so pissed he sent that mutherfucka back to Jersey.)

Tell you what, though, once I finally made it home, I slept like a baby that night.

CHAPTER FOURTEEN

FIGHT NIGHTS

*"Where Death Row went there was drama.
Where there was trouble, there was Death Row."*

I was talking to an associate of Mike Tyson's, before he fought Evander Holyfield for the second time. We'd known each other since I hooked up with Death Row. At one point, I wanted to work for Tyson's camp. He takes very good care of the people he works with, bought them all cars and treated them well. He took good care of them because he was viewing them in the long term, and I liked that about him. I'm a long-term person, myself. My attitude is, if you give me a chance, I'll prove myself to you.

A lot of things have changed for Mike since his last fight, though.

Our mutual friend told me Mike was in the best fighting shape of his life. He'd never been more fit or more prepared to go into the ring. He was on a mission to regain his title from Holyfield, who'd taken it away from him in October 1996, only a month after Tupac's death.

The infamous rematch, where Mike took a bite out of Holyfield's ear, changed his future and the future of boxing.

There've been three really sad, black days for boxing in the past two years. Riddick Bowe fought Andrew Galotta in Madison Square Garden and there was a riot after the fight because Galotta kept hitting Bowe in the nuts, and Bowe's corner jumped in the ring. Then, Oliver McCall had a nervous breakdown in the ring.

Nothing of course, compares to the stunt Mike Tyson pulled. When I watched that fight, I couldn't help but think of Tupac. You see, the two of them were cut from the same cloth and it's the main reason they were such close friends. They understood each other so well, and having worked with

Pac, been around Mike, and experienced the things I've experienced, I understood what was up.

If you could have stopped Mike right dead in his tracks, before he went for Holyfield's ear and said to him: "Mike, you are about to throw away everything you've ever worked for. You'll no longer go down in history a legend. Your family will be affected. You'll never be compared to Muhammad Ali or Joe Frazier anymore. Your historic future will be snatched right out from under you. *Stop right now*."

Do you think you would've have stopped him? No.

Mike would have looked at you, and said, "Get the fuck out my way before I take *your* ear off."

When everybody got in the ring right after, you know what it did? It excited him more—you know why? His animal instincts came out, it was all about survival for him. He said, *Fuck it, I'm not boxing no more. I'm fighting now.* Understand, even though he's been through the system— he's been locked up, locked down, for three years—when he was backed up into that corner, do you think he cared about going back to jail? No. He's looking at the situation like this: *Deal with it when it's over, right now, this is what I want to do.*

That's the way Suge, Tupac, Reggie, and everyone in that whole scene viewed the world around them. *We'll deal with it when the time comes.*

Mike Tyson, Suge Knight, and Tupac Shakur didn't come together accidentally. They subscribed to the same Thug Life ethic and no matter how much Tyson tried to shake those shackles in prison, when he fought Holyfield for the second time, he proved he's still chained to that world psychologically.

Tupac and Tyson got along so well because they were alike in a lot of ways. Mike Tyson was the youngest, baddest black boxer in history, and Tupac was the youngest, baddest black rapper in history. They both had all the fame and glory anyone could achieve in a lifetime, but what did it mean in retrospect? Nothing—it meant nothing. Neither of them could detach their emotions from their professions.

Professionalism would get abandoned, *boom*, at the drop of a hat. When a situation hit, forget about it, they didn't care. The brothas didn't give a fuck about how they'd be perceived. They'd revert right back to where they came from, the streets. If he could've taken his gloves off, he would've fought Holyfield with his fists, because he lost his mind.

When you lose your mind like that, you don't care about your career. Mike didn't care about boxing no more. He cared about the fact that he wanted to fight this guy clean and he got a head-butt, whether it was intentional or not—and in my mind it wasn't—but that's not how Tyson saw it. He went into that fight wanting to regain the championship fairly. He had never been in better shape in his entire life, and he was ready for a muthafuckin' fight. But when Holyfield tied him up and he got head butted again in the second round, what went on in Mike's head was, *Fuck it! It's all out the window. I don't care, I'm just going no-holds-barred, and whatever happens, happens.*

Just like with Tupac. When Pac snapped, he wasn't thinking about consequences, he never did with fighting. He just loved to fight and never cared about getting in trouble. All he wanted to do was get it out of his system. Tyson did the same thing. He felt the fight was dirty and he tried to call the referee over.

Regardless, it's always going to go back to where you came from. You can take the boy out of the hood, but you can't take the hood out of the boy. That's why the two of them were such good friends. They understood one another, and admired each other. Mike Tyson felt the same way about Tupac. When we were on tour in Ohio, Tupac had Mike come up onstage and do a song with him. Mike was wearing a black beanie cap, black gloves, and a leather jacket. Pac started rappin' about Mike, and Mike was jumping up and down on the stage, throwing his hands in the air, and screaming like a bitch, he was so excited.

When he got off the stage, he was standing right by me, saying, "Oh my God, Tupac's the best! He's the greatest rapper in the world." I thought about him saying that to me backstage, and after watching the last fight, all these memories came back to me.

Tupac Shakur needed to fight the way a junkie needs a fix. The only difference is, he was in control over it. But he still liked it. He still needed it. He needed to know he was so controversial he could get into fights and still have people talking about it. He's not as soft as some people might think.

He'd get into fights because niggas talk about shit like that. "Man, I just got back from a video shoot and Tupac got into a fight and he kicked homeboy's ass. You shoulda seen it." It was just something he had a need for. You are as good as the reputation that precedes you. He already had a reputation so he didn't have anything to prove, necessarily. In fact, he was trying to clean that shit up, to some extent. I never got the impression he was out to prove himself.

Aligning yourself with Death Row meant you were ready for drama. That's just how it was. I didn't trip about the fights, because I knew where it was coming from and I figured a lot of this shit was just something they'd outgrow in a few years. They'd realize a beef was nothing to lose your life over, especially when you had so much going for you.

In the meantime, they were always ready to rumble.

One night, we were at the House of Blues for a party after a bunch of college players got drafted into the NFL. The Sunset Strip nightclub is a big-ass place, and it was packed that night. I'd never seen more people squeezed into the club than that night. Everybody was all up on everybody and people were dancing and getting buck-wild, but it never fuckin' fails, as soon as we got there, somebody starts some shit. Somebody always came with drama and it's not like Death Row was always looking for it, or the artists—granted, they never ran from anything, but they didn't always start. The fact is, they were challenged everywhere they went. People were always stepping to them to see what they got. On that night, Snoop, Pac, Suge, Hammer, Six Feet Deep, and all of the security got into it. Even the ballplayers were throwing punches.

The club got closed down and it was big mess. Before it happened, though, Tupac and I got into our own little squabble.

Here's what went down right when Tupac and I showed up. We were on the first level and Pac wanted to make his way the bar. It was packed and when we were in a crowd, Pac was always on my right. I had one hand behind him to keep people from coming up from behind, and I had my left arm in front of him to push people out of his way who might be coming up from the front. We made our way to the bar, and there's a dude standing there. He saw us coming and worked his way over to Pac. He grabbed him from the top of his head, and he started pressing down on him. I saw Pac start talking to him and think, *Okay, I guess he must know him.* But then

I started hearing pieces of the conversation, and it didn't sound right. So I backed the guy up against the bar and say, "Look homie, why don't you back off."

He looked at Pac and said, "What's up with your bodyguard, man, why he trippin'?"

Pac told the dude, "That's my homeboy, man, he's only looking after me."

So we got into a little pushing match, and the dude backed off.

I looked at Pac and said, "Pac, I thought you knew him."

Pac said, "I never seen that nigga in my life."

We started laughing, but the club didn't think it was funny. There were two or three fights that night, and it just got crazier. Before we left, we saw that nigga again and this time he's talking to one of his boys, pointing at me and saying, "That nigga trippin'. A brotha can't even go talk to Pac."

I stepped to him and said: "Listen nigga, I have a job to do and originally I thought you knew Tupac but obviously you don't. So I intervened. Now don't be talking shit to your homeboy as if we did something to you. You're the one who's trippin'."

It wasn't a big deal, but it happened so many times. Everywhere we went, someone was looking to get a piece of Pac. There's so many jealous brothas out there, so many broke-ass niggas who want what he got or who don't think he deserves what he got and the truth is, from knowing him, I can tell you, he earned every damn penny he made and he had more talent than anybody I've ever met. But a lot of people just couldn't handle it.

Every time something went down, I just tried to be me. I'd be professional, I'd try to neutralize the situation before something got out of control. I'd go up to a brotha and try to reason with him first, saying, "I'm Pac's bodyguard, and you're drunk or you're high and we wouldn't even be having this conversation if you were taking care of your business." I'd tell the crew to just ignore whoever it was, telling them the brotha wasn't worth the time. Often I was able to quash things before they got out of hand.

Then there were the times when you couldn't stop things before they escalated. It would be too late. More often than not, Pac saw how I reacted and was down with it. He saw I wasn't afraid to get into any beefs, but as a professional I would try to stop something before it started. If it started, however, I was down. I would do what I had to do.

I had opportunities to prove this over and over again. The night we were at the Le Montrose Hotel in West Hollywood, we had just finished shooting a Dogg Pound video for *Soul Train* and Tupac wanted to kick it there because he heard Total was in town. They're an all-girl group on the Bad Boy label and Pac was trying to track them down because he wanted to fuck one of them. Like I mentioned earlier, the other rumor was Faith was supposed to be in town and he was looking for her, too.

We were camping looking for Faith and Total, and it may sound funny to anybody who didn't know Pac but that fact is, he could pretty much fuck anybody he wanted and he was always on the prowl. We were all upstairs in the room they rented and Pac and his homies were getting high and getting drunk, and the whole room was filled with smoke. I'm out on the balcony and I look down toward the street level and see Yak and Muta downstairs fucking around with the dude who just stepped out of the limo. They were getting real loud and I heard someone scream, so I say to Pac, "I think your Li'l Homies are gettin' into it." By the time Pac got onto the balcony, you could see them pushing and screaming and shit, so we all broke out to the door and everybody ran to the elevator, and I'm yelling, "Fuck the elevator, let's take the stairs!" Pac followed me to the stairwell and we flew down about five flights before landing in the lobby.

But before we even made it out of the room, we had to spring over Big Syke, who'd been sleeping on the floor and jumped up when he heard the commotion. He had a hangnail so he was wearing sandals, and he tripped and fell before making it out the door, and we all had to hurdle over him. It was crazy and, of course, when we got to Muta and Yak, Pac was the first to say, "Yo! What's up . . ." getting in the face of ol' boy who's got the beef with his homies.

I stepped in and started talking to the guy, and suspected Muta and Yak had provoked the shit. His homies knew Pac was always looking for a good fight so they'd instigate 'em sometimes and sure enough, Pac was ready to start swinging.

I size up the situation and realize, the dude's alone and he's a skinny muthafucka and it's not cool to try to take him on without figuring out what went down. I say to Pac, let's just talk to the dude and see what's up.

This time, Pac was real calm and the guy starts talking about knowing Pac from up North and explains that his homeboys started the beef, how it was over some of this dude's bitches. "Pac, I didn't know these were your boys, man," said the dude. "Li'l niggas wanna get tough and shit, I'm just trying to go into the hotel."

Muta and Yak had been talking shit to these two girls and the limo rolled up and he knew the girls, and saw what was going down and talked back to them. He and Pac talked it out and it was cool, and sure enough, we go back to the hotel room and everybody starts replaying the scene, talking about Big Syke laying up in the middle of the floor and how I was the only one with sense to take the stairs. As I listened, I could see a change in Tupac's perception of me.

That was one of the first times we'd been in the mix together, and I could tell by the way he talked about it later, he liked how I handled my business. They saw how I responded and that I was on their side and that I'd try to neutralize a situation but wouldn't stop them from fighting if that's what they had to do.

I also understood their language and their body language. I knew all the signals and I knew all the slang. If you're from the ghetto, you know the dialect and you know the game, and situations that might scare somebody else was just business as usual for me. I wasn't living that lifestyle anymore but I understood it and looked at all the drama as just kids being kids. I'm older and have seen a lot of shit in my day, and nothing was shocking to me.

Nevertheless, drama, drama, drama, was everywhere. After Death Row signed Six Feet Deep, one of its members got into it with some dude, and Suge just happened to be there. When the dude saw Suge coming after him, he said, "Oh shit, Suge, I didn't know these were your boys. If I'd have known that, this never would've happened." Dude apologized, even though supposedly the guy from Six Feet Deep had stolen something from him, but when Suge came into the picture, the whole thing got quashed.

That's another thing, if you were rolling with Death Row, you were rolling with *the* family. It's like you were rolling with Gotti or Scarface or the Untouchables. There was no confusion. When Tupac teamed up with Suge, he knew what he was doing. He was aligning himself with the biggest, baddest brotha out there and he really felt the power. Of course, to obtain power, you're always compromising something and Pac compromised a lot. Some people even think he gave his life. . . .

662

Although there have been a lot reports about the definition of 662, the name of Suge's club in Vegas, which spells MOB on a phone keypad and is linked with Bloods terminology, Tupac had his own definition for MOB: Money Over Bitches.

Anyone who hung out at the club, knew the two went hand in hand. The girls wanted to get into 662 because they wanted to meet the playas with cash. No matter what, something always jumped off at 662. The night Tyson fought Frank Bruno, a huge fight broke out at 662, Suge's club on the Strip. Tupac was right in the middle of it. It usually didn't have anything to do with him; half the time, he just had to get in the mix. On this particular night, every member of security was there. The dude who was in the middle of it was a member of the Wu-Tang Clan. He got his ass *whooped*. Half of the Death Row posse whooped his ass.

I've got Tupac up against a wall. He's jumpin' off the wall, bouncing all up and down in the air, but I have him and he can't get away. He keeps trying to push with one leg, but he was in my arms. Then, our security stepped in and grabbed the guy who was getting the beating, took him to the front door and outside the club. The fuckin' Las Vegas Metro Police whooped this dude's ass again.

After everybody cooled down, I told Pac if he wanted to be mad at me, that was just fine, because I'm not gonna let him get in the middle of this stupid shit. "If you don't want me as your bodyguard, that's fine, too," I told him. "But my job is to protect you and keep you out of trouble."

He said, "Yeah, I know, Frank. I know."

"I'm not gonna let you get in shit, just to get in shit."

"But that was my homeboy, Danny Boy," Pac said.

"You know what, whatever was going on, it's handled."

Tupac was trying to get into the tail end of the fight, anyway. But everybody got their punches in. Reggie was throwing punches, Danny Boy was wailing on the dude.

I'll never forget what Tupac did next. We were in the elevator of the Luxor, heading back up to our rooms, and Tupac was talking to Suge. He said, "Yo Suge, we need to rectify this situation with Ol' boy. It wasn't right how that went down."

I thought to myself, *You gotta be fuckin' kidding. Tupac is saying this?* I must be hearing shit.

So Suge took it to heart, and they quashed it.

It's going to be difficult for a lot of people to understand this point, but I liked Suge Knight, and as you continue to read this book, you'll learn even after all I've been through with Death Row, I still do. I know people who have done a lot worse things than Suge Knight's ever done, and far less good. I know people who have destroyed entire neighborhoods, and Suge wasn't on that level.

One thing I noticed about him early on is he made a point of asking security to step out in certain situations. It wasn't because he didn't trust our loyalty, it was because he had respect for our careers. That may sound crazy, but it's true. He didn't want us to bear witness to events that would compromise our careers. You got to remember, most of the guys who worked for Wrightway were members of the force or off-duty members. The truth is, most of us had been on both sides of the coin, and we weren't going to be ratting Suge for petty bullshit, but he also didn't want anything on our conscience.

In a weird way, we found that respectful.

An L.A. investigator called me up not too long ago, and asked me what I knew about an incident that went down at Death Row's Christmas party in '95. He called both Les and me—at the time, I was talking to the homicide detectives from Las Vegas—and I learned the F.B.I. also wanted to talk to me.

Les and I *heard* the incident, but we didn't see it.

We were at this house in Beverly Hills called the Château, which Suge had rented for the evening, and everyone was partying in Suge's suite. I still have a copy of the invite list, and it reads like a who's who in entertainment. I was standing post outside of Suge's suite, so I don't know who made it to the party, but among those invited were Madonna, Sade, Richard Roundtree, Eric Roberts, Boyz II Men, Little Richard, Bruce Springsteen—the list was eleven pages long. The house was so fuckin' big, there were so many rooms, and the party was going off. They even had a stage and the Whispers performed.

A guy who knew Puffy Combs was upstairs hanging out with Death Row. Another guy was outside on the ground level, and he heard some screaming. When he looked up, there was a guy hanging over the balcony—and members of Death Row were standing there, holding the guy by the ankles. His buddy ran and called for help, but the guy was getting his butt kicked. We didn't see who was doing the beating, your imagination is as good as ours, but we heard they were threatening him to find out where Puffy was living. Apparently this is the reason they were jackin' the guy up in the first place.

I'm not going to make any excuses for the behavior, but I wasn't trippin', either.

It was just another day at the Death Row offices. There were so many incidents, I don't know how anyone can keep track of the pending lawsuits that resulted from a lot of them. Producers disappeared from the studio all the time, Sam Sneed, Johnny J, DJ Quik. Sam Sneed's supposedly in hiding—apparently Pac beat up Sneed in Suge's office once. He was one of the producers, who was there one day and gone the next. Pac punked him in Suge's office, behind the heavy deadbolted door.

I remember one time in New Orleans, we were in Suge's hotel suite, when he asked us to step outside the door, because he needed to handle a situation *internally*.

Unfortunately, the drama was usually caused by somebody saying the wrong thing, and that was all it took.

When Pac was hot, he'd tell you to your face about how he didn't like you, he'd tell you about your momma and everybody else, and *fuck you*. Everything goes back to being a kid. Whatever he had to deal with growing up, whatever he saw, and the shit he went through, it made him angry.

It also made him a poet. That was Tupac's contradiction, and that's what frustrated so many people. They want the good guy or the bad guy and have trouble accepting both.

Poor Les, Tupac usually gave him the bad guy. When they were working on the "Hit 'Em Up" video, at a warehouse off of Slauson Avenue near the Fox Hills Mall, Pac was fuckin' around with someone and Les heard somebody pop off with something to the effect of, "You'll get shot."

Les heard Tupac address the dude with, "Nigga, my bodyguard's standing right there. Les, you got your strap?"

He said, "Twenty-four–seven. . . ."

"Show 'em your strap."

So he lifted up his shirt, and showed them the gun.

Pac said, "See that? That muthafucka'll bust a cap in yo' ass."

This was during the time he was fuckin' around with Salli, and as everyone was getting ready to leave the set, Pac said to Les, "Remember that nigga who was up here fuckin' with my Benz? He just put a secret compartment in my shit where I can hide a secret weapon, and the police would never know it's there."

Les didn't know what he was leading up to.

"Check it out," Pac said, "do you have a gun you can loan me for the night?"

Les flipped out.

"It didn't matter that he was on parole and couldn't be caught near a weapon," says Leslie. "Regardless, Pac was always going to go out fighting. I asked him why he wanted a gun, and he said he was heading over to Salli's pad. I couldn't figure out what he was up to, and I said to him, 'If there's a problem, I'm your bodyguard. Let's roll. I'm the one licensed to carry a gun.' On the other side of the coin, I'm a police officer and my gun is a police weapon, and I knew I couldn't put the gun in his hand. By the same token, if he was having a problem, I told him I'd go with him."

Pac acted like Leslie had betrayed him. In Pac's mind, Les wasn't *down* with him, and he was pissed off.

"What's crazy about the whole thing is, Frank would've done the same thing *but* Pac wouldn't have asked Frank for his gun."

In other words, what Les is trying to say is Tupac punked him. The next day, he told me Les just wanted to find out where Salli lived. I have no doubt Leslie's story is a hundred percent accurate, but the way Pac looked at it, was, "You supposed to be my boy, you're part of my posse and you're not down with me."

Shit had been going on for days, he'd already gotten into with Leslie over the picture he'd taken of Salli, and the bad taste was already in Tupac's mouth. When Leslie didn't give up the gun, it became, *Okay, you're just after my fuckin' woman, you just want to find out where my woman lives.*

It's true Tupac didn't put me in the same compromising positions he put Les in, but he also knew by my actions, I was down for him no matter what—his fights became my fights; his enemies, my enemies. Tupac needed loyalty from the people around him, and he got it from me, straight up. As the song goes from the *Gridlock'd* soundtrack, "Never Had a Friend Like Me."

I don't speak on things I don't know about, so I can't tell you about Pac's childhood. If you're reading this book, you already know something about his youth because you're probably a fan and he told so much about it in his music. Working with him, I knew he lived and breathed Thug Life, and that had to come from somewhere in his heart. For Pac, anyone who turned their back on Thug Life was a sellout muthafucka.

I knew exactly where he was coming from. I was older and had already been through a lot of the shit I watched him go through, but that didn't mean I looked down on the brotha for his struggles. Not at all.

The ironic thing about Pac was he was at peace with himself. He wasn't at peace necessarily with everything going down in the world around him, he couldn't find peace there. He didn't see black people coming together and being one nation. He didn't see them stopping the robbing and the shooting and the things going on among themselves. He couldn't find a way to bring peace to that. He ignored Martin Luther King and Malcolm X and all the other political leaders. He didn't see anything he could do in this lifetime, and even though he felt there would probably be other activists coming up in their footsteps, he didn't see any changes. Pac felt like only God could change the direction of this world, and God wasn't going to step in anytime soon.

Pac is definitely in a better place. I don't care what people say, the negative shit, because I knew the man. It's not like I knew the man that knew the man, I knew the man.

One of his many struggles is people always wanted to challenge him, to push his buttons and see, Was he really a fighter? Working with him, I had the impression that Tupac was a true fighter. He had no fear of anyone. To prove that, I can tell you about the time Tupac wanted to take on me.

You have to understand, I'm a big man. Tupac wasn't even half my size. People don't generally pick fights with me. They avoid starting shit with a brotha like me because I look like I can kick someone's ass and the truth is, I can. The only difference is, I'm older and I don't go looking for shit, so it's not likely shit's gonna come my way.

Pac, on the other hand, did come my way one night and I almost lost it on him. He challenged me one time and didn't even realize he was doing it till later.

It was the last day of shooting on *Gridlock'd*. He was in the best mood that night. He had some women in the trailer, his homies were with him, Salli was history and they were all getting fucked-up. He asked me to get Kevin Hackie into the trailer because he wanted Kevin to do a run for him. Malcolm told Kevin to go get Pac some Hennessey, and he gave him forty bucks.

Kevin went and got the Hennessey and when he got back, he handed me the shit and I took it in to Pac.

Malcolm asked, "Where's the change?"

I said, "He didn't give me any change."

So Pac tells me to get the change from Kevin.

Kevin says, "There ain't no change."

"Hey man," I said. "All I'm doing is delivering the message."

So I went back to Pac and told him what Kevin said, and he told me to get Kevin's ass in the trailer.

I went and got Kevin and told him. Kevin's sitting in the van and it's about midnight, and we're tired, dead fucking tired. We've been on the set for eight weeks, and we're in no mood to have it end this way.

We get back to the trailer and Malcolm opens the door. He asks about the change again.

"What do you mean?" Kevin asked. "The shit cost forty bucks. There's only a dollar and some change."

"I thought you said there wasn't any change!" said Malcolm.

"Here it is!" said Kevin, and he gave whatever he had to Malcolm.

Pac jumped up off the couch and ran to the door. Kevin was on the first step of the trailer and I was at the bottom of the stairs, on the other end of the trailer.

"What the fuck you talkin' about, Hackie!" he screamed. "These are my fuckin' soldiers. If I tell them to do something, they do it. Where's my fuckin' change at?!"

So they start getting into it and it's getting fuckin' serious. He comes out of the trailer and gets right in Kevin's face and he starts screaming at the top of his lungs, "I'll kick both of y'all asses!"

I looked at him, backed up a little bit, shook my head, and said to myself, *No, he did not just say that.*

Pac moves in on Hackie, and says, "I don't give a fuck about y'all being cops. I don't care. I was on fuckin' lockdown. This ain't no fuckin' lockdown. I'll do what the fuck I want to do."

I'm trippin'. This boy's ready to go down, and I'm 'bout to take him there. I'm supposed to go to Italy with him for a week, two days from that night, and I'm thinking, *Fuck it. I'm not going anywhere with this fool.*

By this time, Pac's back in the trailer and Kevin and I look at each other and we head over to where Al Gittens is stationed. He's the supervisor for that night, and I informed him I was leaving.

"Pac's trippin', I'm out."

Kevin said the same thing and we both started walking to our cars.

Al says, "Look, yo, y'all can't do that. *You're* his security guards."

I told him, "Fuck that. I don't let anybody disrespect me like he just did." Kevin felt as strongly as I did.

All of a sudden Muta comes out of the trailer, and says, "Yo Frank, Pac wants you." I thought, *Oh no, here we go. I'm gonna have to set this young nigga straight.* I walk inside and there's smoke everywhere.

I look at Pac, and he's so fucked-up, his eyes are bloodred. Nigga's truly fucked-up.

He's got a drink in his hand, fuckin' bitches everywhere in the trailer. I could tell he was showing off a bit for his audience. Wanted them to see a bit of Thug Life.

I say to him coldly, "Wassup? You wanted to see me."

He looked at me, and said, "Yo Frank, nigga, that wasn't meant for you. As a matter of fact, when I came out the trailer, I was seeing double. I thought someone was standing next to Kevin."

That nigga was so fucked-up, when he came out the trailer saying he would kick both our asses, he thought he was looking at *two* people. That's why I was trippin'. I wasn't gonna even get involved with that shit, I wasn't standing anywhere near Kevin.

He was so fucked-up he saw two Hackies. I'd never seen him that out of it.

He apologized to me and said, "You know you're my homeboy, Frank."

I told him I was about to tell him to find some other brotha to take to Italy, and we started laughing about it, and as I was leaving the trailer, I heard him tell one of the girls who I was.

"See, that there is Big Frank. He's my bodyguard, my homeboy."

＊　　＊　　＊

I was ready to walk out on his ass, but he saved the day. We didn't get out of there till four-thirty A.M. and needless to say, he never apologized to Kevin. They got into it all the time for little shit and that's why he didn't want Kevin as his main bodyguard. He tolerated Kevin, but he didn't like him. He liked the fact Kevin was real militant, knew the law and was ready to pull his gun on someone in a heartbeat, but they weren't quite in step together.

After leaving one of Pac's video shoots, Kevin was following Pac and his homies back from the set and they got into it with some muthafuckas on the Sunset Strip. They pulled over at a convenience store, and Kevin told me the next day, he had to draw down on the niggas. He called the sheriff, they showed up, and it was handled.

I called Reggie to see what he'd heard, and he told me, "Man, Frank, I wish you'd been with Pac. Hackie pulled his gun. I even told him, 'If it had been Frank, it never would've happened. Frank would've talked the muthafuckas out of doing something foolish.' "

I'd had luck talking our way out of situations before, but I don't know if I would've been able to handle this one any differently.

The fact was, the situations surrounding Tupac kept getting deeper and deeper all the time, and it became more and more apparent we were all in over our heads.

CHAPTER FIFTEEN

HIT 'EM UP

For all the security meetings we had, and there were a lot of them, important shit wouldn't get done. From my perspective, Wrightway did not always pay close attention to what was going down in the studio. We should've been warned about "Hit 'Em Up," a controversial song Tupac recorded that basically invited drama from the East Coast.

At the very least, they might have considered warning me, his bodyguard. I understood why Pac hadn't said anything, he just created shit, he didn't sit around and talk about it. But I hadn't been warned at all, and I'm driving my car one day in June, my wife and I had gone out to dinner and we're on our way home, listening to Julio G on The Beat. I heard a new Tupac song come on, but then Julio started *bleepin', bleepin', bleepin'.* The song was *bleepin'* more than it was playing. My wife and I were sitting in the driveway, listening to it in disbelief. By the time I walked in the door, my phone was already ringing and it was Reggie, asking me if I heard the song.

I told him, "Reggie, we are going to need two bulletproof vests, we're gonna need to have more than me as a bodyguard for Pac, and you know that. I'm going to talk to Pac, and we need to talk to Suge." Depending on what functions we were going to, I wore a vest now, but Pac rarely did and shit was going to have to change.

The song basically attacks the Bad Boy camp, from Biggie Smalls to Puffy Combs, and everyone on their side. "Hit 'Em Up," was basically referring to, "*When we see you, we're bringing drama, fist to fist, glove to glove, gun, whatever. If you see us, you better be ready to throw down because it's on.*"

When I went into the trailer the next day, I looked at him and said, "What the fuck are you doing?"

He looked at me and goes, "What?" And then he starts laughing, that mischievous Pac giggle. He was standing there, without a shirt on, smoking a blunt in the back of the trailer.

"Nigga, I gotta get two vests now," I said. "On the real, Pac, you need to talk to Suge. We got to up your security. This song is gonna create a lot of shit, and there's gonna be a lot of places we're going, where you're gonna need more than just one set of eyes."

Pac walked toward the stereo and put the fuckin' song on, and when he came toward me, he started rapping to it. I couldn't believe this boy.

When he finished rapping, he said, "Frank, this song is going to be playing in every club, all over. Deejays are calling from everywhere, wanting to get a piece of this!" The song wasn't on an album, it was the B-side to the "How Do U Want It" single. It wasn't scheduled to be released for a while and already it was off the hook.

I repeated my feelings about it, and he just said, "Call Reggie."

I told him I talked to him last night, and he had said, "Call Suge."

He didn't seem to give a fuck, but he wasn't against me trying to get additional help.

Okay, I'm thinking, *now I'm finally going to get the extra security I need to keep this boy out of trouble.*

Wrightway had meetings all the time with Suge at his house in Malibu, and we called one over this song. The meeting was supposed to start at eleven P.M., but Suge didn't show up till two A.M. I knew we in for some trouble because we had New York shows coming up, we were getting ready to travel to various places, I knew there would be people on the West Coast who weren't going to appreciate that song, and I voiced my concern about it. I told Suge directly, "We need more guards working with Pac."

"Yeah, you're right," he said. "But he don't like anybody but you."

I was surprised to hear him say that in front of everybody else, but I was also glad to hear he agreed with me. The truth was, there were about fifteen guards in the room that night, and when that song came out, none of them wanted to go near Pac. Most of these guys found him difficult to work with to begin with, and now it wasn't gonna get any easier. As I think about it now, "Hit 'Em Up" was a bad-luck song from the first time I heard it. If you think about it, look what happened just a short time later. I guess my gut feeling was right.

Suge must have known how serious the problem was. It should have been a priority for the entire company, but it seemed that I'm the only one who viewed it that way. Obviously, they weren't thinking about what would happen if they lost him. They were Death Row, and they just weren't taking this shit seriously. Even the song ends with a line about how the D.R. staff comes strapped.

The irony is, Suge knew the importance of security. He praised security all the time, telling us without security, there's no Death Row because we were in charge of the artists, the studio, and we helped run the company. If we were having problems with artists, he wanted to know about it.

I remember one time, he called a meeting at Gladstone's, a fish restaurant in Malibu overlooking the Pacific Ocean, and every swinging dick from Death Row was there, from the office to the studio. He ripped assholes up and down that night. The point of the meeting was Death Row was moving forward, and he felt people were undermining him, which to Suge was like taking food from his hand. He'd found an employee was skimming and he confronted him right there on the spot. The only members of Death Row he praised, was security, because he'd never had problems with us. This was, of course, before Tupac's death. It was also the first night we got to see the art for the *Makaveli* album art, which had Tupac in a Christlike pose on a cross, with the names of every major ghetto city taped to the cross.

Maybe he wasn't Jesus Christ on this earth, but he was someone who needed protection in this world. The trouble is, no one could protect him from himself.

CHAPTER SIXTEEN

LEMIKA

My niece, Lemika Early, had one idol in her life. Like a lot of young black girls, her idol was Janet Jackson. She had Janet's pictures on her walls, all of Janet's records, and even a scrapbook filled with Janet memorabilia. She loved and admired her completely. My niece was also in a wheelchair. In 1995, she and two of her friends were in a terrible car accident, and from the age of fourteen on, Lemika was paralyzed from the waist down. At the hospital, she learned about the Make-A-Wish Foundation, and she got the opportunity to make a wish.

She dreamed of meeting Janet Jackson.

The Foundation arranged everything. Lemika and her entire family were invited to come to Los Angeles in June of 1996. The plans included the chance to spend a half hour with Janet and a trip to Disneyland for the whole family.

I can't tell you how excited everybody was. It's all they could talk about. My niece had never been outside of Chicago and she was getting the chance to spend four nights and five days in L.A. My sister Beverly called me up and told me the news. She'd gone out and bought the family new clothes and everybody was just waiting for the designated day when they were gonna get on that plane.

I'll let Beverly and Lemika tell you what happened.

"At the last minute, they called and said Janet Jackson wanted to change the plans," said Beverly. "I couldn't believe it. They told us we were going to New York instead.

"I said, 'New York? What are we gonna do in New York?' The kids already had their hearts set on California. I'd already spent money on clothes, and with four kids, that's a lot of money."

Lemika was gonna be crushed. It's bad enough she's had to go through the accident, and lose the use of her legs, spending the better part of two years in physical therapy. Now her wish didn't look like it was going to come through, either.

"The lady told me, 'Well, you can visit the Statue of Liberty,' " said Beverly. "I said, 'Hell no, we ain't going to no New York to visit no Statue of Liberty.' We can read about it in a social-studies book. Janet Jackson pissed me off. They said something about Janet had a favorite candy store in New York we could go to, I didn't know what the fuck they were talking about. All I know is, I have a five-year-old daughter, too, who had her heart set on going to Disneyland, and it was turning into a big mess. This all came down at the last minute."

"I was so disappointed," says Lemika. "I was her number one fan, and it meant a lot to be granted that wish."

Working with Pac, I understand a celebrity's busy schedule, but if you're not game to do something, don't say you're gonna do it. Simple as that.

Beverly told the lady she was going to talk to Lemika when she came home from school.

Lemika had to make the decision. All we knew for sure was, Janet Jackson might spend anywhere from fifteen minutes to an hour with her, and was it still worth it to her?

She decided no, it wasn't worth it. When the lady called back, Lemika told her she wanted to go to California.

That's when they called me. I was working on the set of *Gridlock'd*, and Beverly filled me in on everything that happened.

When I went to work the next day, I told Pac the story. I'd never told him anything personal about my family before, and I shared with him everything that had happened to Lemika. Then I told him about Janet Jackson's actions.

We were inside the trailer, and I'll never forget what he said.

"I hate that shit," were his exact words. "What can I do?"

I hadn't even asked him to help out yet, because they were still going to be able to go to Disneyland, and I knew he was busy.

But just like Pac, he was ready to take on more.

I said, "Maybe we can just call my sister and my niece and you can talk to them." That alone would have been a nice gesture.

He said, "Go ahead. Make the call." He handed me his cell phone.

I called Beverly, and told her Pac wanted to talk to Lemika.

"She wasn't home from school yet, and I asked him if he could call back in twenty minutes," says Beverly. "He called back exactly twenty minutes later."

"I was shocked," says Lemika. "I didn't think I'd get to talk to Tupac, but Uncle Frankie had *pub*."

Everybody in the house was crying. I could hear it in the background. Lemika had been having a really hard time, and he made her feel so much better.

"She was walking on clouds," says Beverly.

As soon as Tupac hung up the phone with her, he asked me what size clothes she wore. I told him I didn't know, and he told me to call Yaasmyn at his office, and give her my sister's phone number and have them send Lemika anything and everything that she wants.

Mind you, he'd never met her, it was the first time they had spoken, and he was doing this out of the kindness of his heart.

My family was floored. But it gets better.

My family flew into California, and Tupac invited them to the set of *Gridlock'd*. He told them to take all the pictures they wanted, and he gave Lemika a blanket that belonged to him. He used that blanket every day on the set and she clung to it. "I nearly caught hell when I washed it," says Beverly. "She had spilled something on it, and I put it in the washing machine. I thought she was never gonna forgive me."

There was a whole crew of people. The kids each had a friend along, and her husband brought a buddy of his. Pac was so cool. He wasn't bothered at all. He even invited them to a barbecue at his house, and when he found out my brother-in-law, William, played basketball, he ordered an entire basketball court down to the set. They took a million pictures.

Believe it or not, it gets even better.

Tupac invited them all down to the studio the next day. He had some recording to do. At the studio, they got to meet Snoop Dogg, Danny Boy, Kurupt, and everybody who was working for Death Row that day.

"It was my husband's friend's birthday," says Beverly. "And Tupac told us to order anything we wanted to eat, have whatever we wanted to drink, anything we wanted."

Pac ordered about ten pizzas.

I have most of the time we spent in the studio on videotape, and every now and then, I watch the tape again. Pac's got a joint dangling from his lips most of the time, dressed casually in a button-down silk shirt and white pants. To watch him is to remember how damn funny he was.

At one point, one of the runners, James, walked in wearing a tank-top jersey, and Pac starts clowning him about a Chinese-looking tattoo he's got on his arm.

"Nigga's gettin' Chinese letters like he's been somewhere, shit, you ain't never left the block."

Pac points to the tattoo and looks dead in the camera. "You know what this says? 'Two egg rolls with hot sauce, to go.' "

Everybody in the studio started cracking up, and you can hear my voice saying, "Pac, you missed your calling. Shoulda been a comedian."

A couple minutes later Pac hears Lemika calling me "Frankie," and he starts clowning *me*.

"Frank-E, Frank-E Knuckles. I'm gonna call him Frank-E, now, cuz the 'E' is for Extra Sexy!"

He starts singing to the tune of the Right Said Fred song, "Catwalk." *"Frank-E's too sexy for some sleeves, too sexy for some pants . . ."* Man, he was funny that day, and everybody had a great time. He even put Lemika's voice on one of the tracks.

"She gave Hanover Park, the area where she's from, a shout-out," says Beverly. "We all couldn't believe it. When it was time to leave, he came outside with us and gave us all hugs, like we were family." Before they left, Tupac gave Lemika his driver's license. It was just about to expire, his birthday is June 16, and he wanted to give her something special.

I didn't know about this until about a year later, but before they all left the studio that day, Tupac told William I was like a brother to him, and my family was his family.

"Everything he did for us came out of a love for Frankie," says William. "He told me when we were at the studio, that him and Frankie were like brothers, and the love he had for Frank flowed over to us."

I cried when I heard that, because I always felt like he had a special place in his heart for me, but until William told me what Pac said, I didn't know he ever voiced how he felt. Pac wasn't that kind of man, and neither am I.

I still get choked up thinking about the love he showed my family. For everything you read about Pac in the tabloids, he had a beautiful heart and he shared it with those he loved.

"This man was nothing like they say he was," says Beverly. "He couldn't do enough for us. He had plans to donate a stereo system to Lemika's high school. He told her he was going to bring something back from Italy, and he told her just to hang in there and be strong, that he'd never forget about her. He even said he was going to put her in his next video, and that it was going to be a children's video. I believe he meant it."

Everything had worked out better than they could have hoped for.

"We weren't even guaranteed a half hour with Janet Jackson, and Tupac spent two days with us, that we'll never forget," says Beverly. I remember Beverly telling me that Lemika once spent an afternoon crying when she found out Janet Jackson collapsed onstage somewhere. Before the Make-A-Wish incident, her fondness for Janet was deep. Now, the pictures she has on her wall have all been replaced with pictures of Tupac.

Till this day, Lemika gets so mad when she hears something negative about Pac. "Television only shows the bad side of him," she says. "That's not the Tupac I met. I got to know him as a person, and he was a beautiful person."

Now, she has one final wish. "I wish I could talk to him in heaven right now," she says. "I'd tell him I love him, and I want to thank him for all the kindness he showed me and my family."

After they left to go back to Chicago, I realized if everyone on this earth had the chance to spend a couple days with him and see that side of him, the public perception of Pac would have changed considerably. To be sure, he was complicated, but he was essentially a good person.

Now it's too late.

PART FIVE

DEATH IN VEGAS

CHAPTER SEVENTEEN

LAS VEGAS, NEVADA, SEPTEMBER 7, 1996

There have been so many questions surrounding the events leading up to Tupac's death, and the truth is, many of the stories reported have been inaccurate. I was with Tupac all day, and all night. I stayed with him in the hospital until Friday, September 13, the day we all lost him.

What follows is a detailed account of what went down in Las Vegas, Nevada, on that dark day.

Vegas was hot, but I wasn't complaining. I was gonna see Pac. While driving in from L.A. the day before, I realized I'd missed the homie. It was my first day back at work from vacation, I'd spent most of August with my ten-year-old daughter, and I looked forward to going back to work. I was scheduled to bodyguard him through the weekend. Tupac was supposed to turn up at the Luxor Hotel sometime in the afternoon, which was just as well because I had a security meeting early in the day, and I didn't want it to conflict with his arrival.

The meeting was held at a Vegas attorney's office. Seems that for proper Nevada state procedure to get clearance for the security officers to carry guns, a letter should have been sent in advance, requesting we be allowed to carry guns. It was not done. No guns meant a lack of security. At the meeting, the attorney confirmed we were not allowed to carry guns on us at any time—especially at the club. Suge had gotten the Vegas police to agree to let him open Club 662 for the night but that didn't mean they were happy about it. If we were caught with a gun on us behind state lines, that's all it would have taken for them to shut 662 down. It didn't matter that out of the twenty guards on duty that night, most were police officers and all were legally licensed to carry weapons. Death Row couldn't take any chances.

The only way Suge got Metro to allow him to have his club open that night, was because it was a benefit for some retired boxer. Once they got benefit status, he was allowed to open it. He wouldn't have been able to swing it any other way, because he was having too many legal problems.

It was, after all, Suge Knight's club and anything related to Death Row didn't particularly thrill them. We'd hired extra security for the post-fight show that night. Run-D.M.C. was scheduled to perform and if the last 662 performance was any indication, we could easily lose control of the crowd.

Shit, when Tupac performed at 662 in November—his first show after he got out of prison—the place got crazy. It was complete chaos. The club's capacity is 680 but there were more than 1,000 fans that night. It was slamming but it was also out of control. Tupac, followed by Suge, David Kenner and the entire Death Row entourage, showed up late in his black Mercedes 500SL, wearing a derby hat and a vest, all charged-up to perform. Mike Tyson was there with his bodyguards, along with Dion Sanders and his entourage, and Forest Whitaker, who was drunk off his ass. Everybody who was anybody wanted in that night.

Tonight, we really had to iron out security detail. The main objective was to keep the crowd under control. They didn't want any problems, because the Las Vegas police department would shut the joint down if you dropped a match. All the rules had to be strictly enforced, and for this evening, that included leaving our guns behind. Like anyone who carries a weapon, I didn't like being without it. It made me feel empty to be without my piece, a compact Colt .45—a police officer's special—that I always took with me on the job. I was never without it, I always had it on me, always, but on this one particular day, I was told to leave it in my car. We were traveling in an entourage that night, so the chances of something happening were slim. That's what I thought.

After the meeting, I caught a ride with Reggie, he took us out to lunch at T.G.I.F.'s. When we finished eating, Reggie started bitching about Kevin Hackie, the bodyguard who replaced me when I was on vacation. They'd gotten into it over money. Kevin, who had worked with Reggie long before he hooked up with Suge to form Wrightway, when they were both policing the streets of Compton, managed to hook something up with the producers of *Gang-Related*, the movie Pac made in August. He got paid $10,000 for offering his technical advice on the shooting scenes. Reggie felt Kevin had undermined his authority by taking the ten grand, and still taking money from Wrightway for bodyguarding Pac. In my opinion, Kevin took what he deserved, but Reggie didn't see it that way.

By now, we were at a carwash down the street from the Luxor on Flamingo Road. Reggie was spilling his guts about Kevin, and I was hearing him out, but I couldn't help but think about Norris Anderson's nickname for Reggie. He used to call him "Rona Barrett," because he talked so much. Norris was married to Suge's sister, and a Death Row executive. I listened to Reggie bitch all the way back to the Luxor.

As soon as we got back to the Luxor, I didn't have any trouble locating Pac. The boy loved to gamble, and to find him, I just looked for the craps table surrounded by the highest percentage of hoochies. Kidada was up in her hotel room. As usual, his soldiers were right by his side.

I made my way over to his table.

Pac lit up when he saw me.

"Big Frank, what's up?" Pac always greeted me warmly, but this time, I could tell he was particularly glad to see me, too. We all embraced—it had been a long month.

Pac was looking good. He was still skinny as all hell, he'd been working for a year straight with little let-up and it was taking its toll on him physically. He was sporting one of the new silky button-down shirts he'd gotten from one of the fashion designers when we were in Italy. More notably, he was boasting a new chunk of gold. A $30,000 diamond-studded medallion about three inches in diameter dangled prominently from his neck. In the middle, it had the emblem for Euphanasia, the name of the company Pac had started. The image was of a muscular, black angel of death, on his knees with his head tilted down and backed by huge wings and a halo. Pac and his crew always spelled names their own way and Euphanasia was his take on "euthanasia," which means an easy and painless death, or a way to end suffering painlessly.

I could tell he was really relaxed and up—he was always in good spirits on fight nights 'cause Tyson was his boy.

The Luxor, however, wasn't treating him right—he was playing at a $25 table and he was losing. Pac was a big bettor and this table wasn't paying off so we decided to move things over to the MGM. It was about two or three P.M. and we had plenty of time to gamble before meeting up with Suge later for the fight.

While we walked over to the MGM, you could already tell it was a fight night. All the rich people were in town—sports heroes, celebrities, high rollers. You could almost feel the money changing hands. We strolled over the bridge separating the two casinos, and when we got to the MGM Grand, Tupac's luck started to change. He began winning big. He was covering all the odds and was coming away with $1,400 to $2,000 a roll. He probably rolled the dice for two or three minutes—a long time on a craps table. Winners always attract a crowd, but as soon as people started figuring out who he was, the crowd got more serious. Tupac loved the attention. What better place for a high-roller gangsta to be seen rolling high, than in Vegas at a craps table?

I started tensing up because everyone was looking to get in his face. Michael Moore had walked with us from the Luxor, and he had Pac flanked on one side and I had the other. The Outlaws were staggered throughout the crowd, spread out so people wouldn't know who they were.

Despite the size of the throng, everything was cool for a while. When Tupac was in a good mood, everything usually stayed pretty cool. It helped that he was on a winning streak, because the Vegas code dictates you don't disturb gamblers in action. But since it was Pac, people were still trying to angle their way in. Dozens of hoochies were hitting him up for an autograph, a photograph, any piece of Pac.

It started getting more and more difficult to keep people out of his space, and it was getting close to fight time. I needed a phone to check in with Reggie at the Luxor, in case Suge was looking for him—he always wanted to know where Pac was at all times. The fucked-up thing was, I didn't have my security staff radio–cell phone. While I was vacation, Kevin used it and since he and Reggie were fighting, I didn't have it on me, because Kevin wasn't coming to Vegas.

I couldn't believe I'm rolling with Death Row's million-dollar boy, one of the biggest rap stars in the world, and I got to use a pay phone. I must've left him for about a minute, long enough to leave Reggie a message from a public phone a couple of feet away, before working my way back to the table.

Pac wasn't there.

Goddammit, I thought to myself, *he's not being security-conscious.* All of them had taken off, leaving me behind, and I had no idea where they'd gone. To top it off, I was stuck without a phone for the night, and I started to get more and more uneasy.

I circled the casino a couple of times, before making the decision to walk back to the Luxor. If I had the radio, I could've reached anybody in security immediately and told them Pac had disappeared.

I felt myself starting to panic. *Pac's been kidnapped. I lost him, it's my fault.*

Dammit, where the fuck is he?

As soon as I got to the Luxor, I began paging him repeatedly. I paged Michael Moore; I tried reaching Reggie. Where was everybody?

Here I am, the number one guy, and I lose Pac making a phone call five feet from him. It was the first time he'd ever left me, and it gave me an eerie feeling. My client had never been missing before.

"Big Frank!" I hear Pac's voice behind me.

A wave of relief passed over me. "Pac, where the hell you all been, man? You left me over there."

"Oh, I asked them where you were at," he said. "Now I can't find anybody."

Tupac Shakur, one of the most wanted men in America, had spent the last hour walking around Vegas alone.

Even the Outlaws were nowhere to be found.

"Ah, Frankie, you know I can kick anybody's ass down here," Pac boasted.

"Dude, you cannot be doing this," I told him. "You can not be shaking security, especially me, especially here in Las Vegas."

"I ain't worried about it."

"Pac, that ain't the point. I know you can fight. The point is, you need security to step in and stop things before they happen. Do me a favor, don't shake me anymore. Do not leave me without knowing where you're at."

For all his bravado, he seemed distracted. It really appeared to bother him that the Outlaws were missing. He called them about a half dozen times but couldn't reach them. The whole thing was odd, because they were always with him. He was like a pissed-off dad whose kids had run off to play.

We sat down near a house phone and waited for someone to turn up.

After another attempt to reach Reggie, we managed to hook up. He told us Suge would meet us at the MGM before the fight. It was too hot to make that walk again so we decided to catch a cab. I looked at Pac, who hadn't changed his clothes since we met at the casino. As usual, he's not wearing his bulletproof vest. It didn't surprise me. Nine times out of ten he didn't wear it. It was always an issue between the two of us. But Pac did what Pac wanted to do. Before the cabdriver could find a place to let us out, I sized up the crowd. It was out of control.

As soon as Tupac got out, people started coming at us from all angles. *"Tupac! Tupac! Tupac! Tupac!"*

I'm all that stands between him and them.

As we're walking through the mob, people started following us, screaming for autographs. I flagged down a MGM security guard, who could clearly see we were having problems. He escorted us behind the crowd out of the view of the aisle to a private lobby near the entrance of the fight area. We hung out there for a while, and as the fight began drawing closer, I watched Tupac begin losing patience.

"I hate this shit. Suge does this all the time."

It was fifteen minutes before fight time and Tupac was getting restless. The prefights were over and Tyson and Seldon were up next.

"Fuck this shit, every time we go somewhere, he always has to be fucking late!" Tupac's eyes were blazing. "I didn't want to come to Vegas, no fuckin' way. We gonna miss the fucking fight."

Despite security efforts to keep crowds away from him, fans kept working their way toward him, taking pictures, asking for more autographs. I watched him get visibly more tense as each minute ticked by.

"Go call Reggie and find out where he is."

I took off toward a phone knowing that he knew and I knew it wouldn't do a damn bit of good. Suge always made him wait and this night was no different. I made the call anyway, a thinly veiled token attempt to ease Pac's tension. Waiting on Suge was a recurring problem. We'd call a meeting and wait three, four, sometimes five hours for Suge to show up. The fact that this was a Tyson fight apparently didn't make any difference.

"I'm gonna get my own goddamn tickets," Tupac said. But we both knew the truth: We weren't going anywhere. We were gonna do what we always did—wait on Suge.

When he finally arrived, it was just him and one of his homeboys. He pulled out four tickets to get us in, and as we were entering, the National Anthem was playing. Security held us up, but Suge and Pac continued to walk toward the ringside seats.

"You're not going anywhere till we let you go by," said one of the officers.

Oh no, here we go already. Suge and Pac started getting hotheaded, and I was foreseeing the first fight of the night. Luckily the anthem ended before they blew up, and we made it down the aisle to watch the fight. Which seemed to last about a minute.

No matter to Pac. He was jumping around hysterically because Tyson took him out so fast.

"Fifty blows! Fifty blows! I counted them, I counted them," he said, jumping up and down with a pugilist's pantomime. "He hit him fifty times. *Bang bang bang bang bang . . . Boom!*"

With Pac leading the pack, we worked our way backstage, and started to mingle with the Tyson camp. We were only there for a couple of minutes before Suge gave the word to leave. This was the first time Pac wouldn't be allowed to greet Tyson, which he did after every fight.

I started to mull over the day, and I realized everything seemed just a beat off. I didn't have my phone, I couldn't carry a gun, Pac had left me and then lost his boys. I started getting a strong premonition that a long night lay ahead of us.

As we exited the backstage area, we met up with the rest of the entourage, which included all of Suge's homeboys and all of Pac's Outlaws. Everyone was crowding around the entrance area, and as we were standing around bullshitting about the fight, Travon—one of Suge's homeboys—came up to Pac and whispered in his left ear.

What he whispered, I don't know, but my heart sunk. It really was gonna be one of those nights.

Like lightning, Pac took off running, and I took off running behind him.

Orlando Anderson—I would learn his name later—stood about six feet one, and it looked like he was anticipating the arrival of someone. Not necessarily Tupac, but someone. He was standing with an MGM security guard, who appeared to have him detained.

Tupac started swinging and Anderson went down immediately. As he fell to the ground, the entire Death Row entourage showed up. At that point, I was pulling Tupac away from Orlando, trying to get him off of him.

Pac's black angel intervened. A link on his medallion broke and he stopped beating on Orlando when the necklace snapped apart. While he went down to grab it, I grabbed him and pulled him away from the scene. I pushed him away from the scuffle, and had him up against a wall.

"Goddammit, Pac, you know you can't be doing this!" I told him. "I'm not gonna let you back over there. Use your head! You've got a court date coming up."

My back was to the fight, but I could hear security coming up. I started easing Tupac out of the picture. My whole objective was to keep him out of it, but he wanted back in. As he attempted to jump back into the crowd, I reached into the fray and plucked him out a second time. At this point, I could see Suge and his homeboys kicking Anderson while he was still down.

"Let's go," I heard Suge yell, and everybody started to scatter. The only problem was, no one knew which way was out and people started to panic. I had scoped out the exits earlier when I was looking for Pac, and knew where to find the nearest door. The crowd saw us head outside, and followed us out of the building.

As we made it to the exit, I could hear security calling for Metro. We proceeded to go back to the Luxor by foot, and as we were walking, everyone's talking about the fight. Tupac didn't waste any time chiming in. The bragging started before we even hit the bridge.

"It was just like the fight. *Boom, one, boom, two, and he was down. I took him out faster than Tyson!*"

Everyone was laughing and congratulating him and no one asked why he beat on the guy. For his part, Tupac didn't offer an explanation. It didn't matter to him why he did it. It was just another fight—another chance for him to prove himself. For Pac, braggin' after a fight, was like having a smoke after sex. He'd get all charged up, and I just looked at his behavior as another part of Thug Life. At the time, all I was thinking was *Thank God we got out of there.*

By now, we probably had at least a hundred groupies following us back over to the Luxor. Men and women, young and old, every kind of hanger-on you could imagine. I was the only bodyguard. Everyone else had their instructions to head over to 662 and no one in security knew what just happened.

I'm on Tupac like glue now. When he went upstairs to change, I went with him.

While Tupac switched out of his jeans and into a pair of green sweat pants and a matching green jersey, I fixed the link on his medallion 'cause he wanted it to wear it out. I sat down in front of the air conditioner, and started chugging on some Hi-C. I realize I was dehydrated from all the commotion.

I began thinking about what just happened. *Oh well*, I tell myself, *it was just another fight, and it's over. We're out of harm's way, and it's done.* It was just like every other fight we'd had in the past, except we didn't get stopped by the police. There were no witnesses, no guns drawn. At this point, I'm not thinking about the cameras, and what they might have captured on video.

I didn't know till later in the week, that the guy he beat up was a Compton Crip they believed tore up a Foot Locker in the Lakewood Mall after trying to snatch Travon's Death Row necklace. Apparently there was a $10,000 bounty for them.

None of this would come to light until much later. In the meantime, all I was thinking about was making it through the rest of the evening with no more bullshit.

While the rest of the world was talking about the Tyson fight—did Seldon take a dive or did he take a punch—Pac continued to talk about the night's real fight. As usual, Kidada missed all the excitement, and he had to fill her in. She laughed at his description of the fight, she loved his roughneck side, and this was as close to the action as she usually got. He didn't invite her to the club tonight, either.

We went back downstairs to the valet parking area, and it was a complete and total scene. The Death Row entourage was in effect. People were getting in cars and heading over to 662, and girls were making their way over to us. Okay, you wanna see some hoochies, here they were. There's nothing like fight-night hoochies. These women put on the skimpiest outfits possible, most of them were half-dressed, with their breasts hanging out and asses hanging out, all angling to get into 662.

None of our entourage was in a hurry to get to the club, least of all Suge. He liked making showy entrances and he wasn't about to arrive early.

Finally, Suge signaled it was time to go to his house, and Pac pulled me aside.

"I want you to drive Kidada's Lexus with the Li'l Homies, and I'm gonna ride with Suge."

My gun was in my car, a two-seater parked on the other side of the hotel, and I knew I couldn't say, *"Hey, Suge, Pac, why don't you wait up a minute while I go over to my car?"* It wouldn't happen. Once we're rolling, we're rolling—there's no time to make a run. I wasn't allowed to carry a firearm tonight anyway, I told myself, and there's going to be twenty security guards waiting at the club by the time we get there. Besides, Pac wants me to do him a favor and look after his Outlaws. Most of 'em can't drive legally, and Pac knew they were gonna get drunk. Somebody had to drive. I wasn't worried. We'd make our way from the hotel to Suge's and on to the club like we had many times before.

As soon as I got in the Lexus, however, another red flag went up. The light was on that indicated the tank was on empty. I had no idea how much reserve Kidada's car had, and I knew damn well we weren't gonna be stopping for gas.

I had to pray we'd make it to Suge's and to the club, because we wouldn't be able to gas up until the evening was over. To make matters worse, Suge had a lead foot—nearly as bad as Tupac's—and I was chasing him on fumes. The capper: I had to keep the windows down because we couldn't risk running the A.C.

Suge's house was a sprawling one-level mansion across from Mike Tyson's and Wayne Newton's homes. Like everything Suge owned, it was dominated by the color red—red carpeting in the master bedroom, red fixtures throughout. It looked the same as it always did, but one detail stood out: since the last time I was there, Suge had had the pool painted a deep bloodred.

At the depths of it was a reproduction of the Death Row emblem.

We only stayed there for about ten or fifteen minutes, before the cars started lining up to head into town. This was a sight to see—a parade of some of the most badass gangbangers around. The entourage consisted of about a dozen cars, all top-of-the-line Mercedes, BMWs, Cadillacs, and Lexuses, and nearly all in black. Suge's homies were all Compton street thugs, afraid of nothing and nobody. As we were taking off, you could hear the Pioneer systems bumping that bass so loud the ground was trembling.

Right as we were nearing the Strip, a bicycle cop motioned Suge to pull over. My windows were down, and I could hear them bumping *Makaveli*, Pac's latest project—Pac always listened to Pac when he was driving; he used the time to review whatever he was currently working on. It seemed the cop had given it a thumbs-down: They were playing the music louder than city limits allowed. Suge was driving a brand-new 750IL that he'd just bought the week before and he hadn't even put in his custom stereo yet. The car didn't have plates, it had come straight from the dealer. The officer asked Suge to step out of the car. I was right on their tail and I could see Suge get out of the car and walk toward the back. He seemed to be relaxed as he opened the trunk and so did the cop. Suge got back in the car and that was the end of it.

I don't know how they managed to avoid being busted for marijuana. It didn't matter that both of them were on probation, Pac had dope on him twenty-four hours a day. His mind-set was, "I'm a multimillionaire, I have the best attorneys in the country, I've got more cash in my pocket than you'll see in a year, so fuck 'em." They didn't take this shit seriously. Their lifestyle, and the way they view pot is, it's a minor offense.

Until I saw Suge drive off, I was sweating it, literally. Between them messing with the police, no A.C., and no gas, I had plenty to be worried about.

At this point, I wanted to suggest to Suge to make a right turn on Tropicana, so we could enter the club the back way, and the only reason I didn't is he'd already blown through the light. He was moving too fast. Suge knew the shortcut, too, and if we were just going to the club to check things out during the day, he would have taken it. But he took Flamingo to make his presence known. They had *Makaveli* blaring, an entourage of cars, and Tyson had won. To top it off, they'd won their own fight and were probably feeling extra good.

As we were cruising down Flamingo, women were rolling up beside the cars and joining in on the entourage. Everyone wanted into the club tonight, and that's how many of them usually got in—by sliding in with us. Crowds of cars started surrounding us, and I started to get the same feeling I had at the casino when Pac was on a winning streak. All eyes were on him and at any moment, things could have sprung out of control.

As we stopped at a red light, a white Cadillac rolled up next to us. I can still see the car clearly, it had the distinctive brake-light configuration that all new-model Caddies have.

I replay that image over and over in my head. It was just another red light, and it was just another white Cadillac. Suge's homie K-Dove was traveling in front of them, and I am directly behind them.

I looked dead at the car, and I saw the arm come out and the gun.

Bam bam bam bam!

My first reaction, was *Oh my fuckin' God.*

I jumped out of the car, and as I was running up to Suge's BMW, the white Cadillac sped off and made a turn to the right. As I reached the BMW, teary-eyed and in shock, I'm thinking, *They're dead. They are dead. There's absolutely no way that anyone in the car's moving.*

Before I made it to the back of the car, the BMW took off and did a U-turn to the left. K-Dove also whipped a U-turn, and I ran back to the Lexus, jumped in, and began following them.

I can't even tell you how fast we were going. We jumped every median getting back to the Strip and we caught up with Suge's car at Vegas Boulevard and Harmon. It had made it through the intersection but was grounded by two flat tires from hitting the medians.

I jumped out of the car and saw that Vegas PD were everywhere. I ran up and identified myself as Tupac's bodyguard and an ex-cop, and they allowed me to come in. Everyone was trying to get at the car but the cops were containing the crowd.

I couldn't believe my eyes. What the fuck was Suge doing spread-eagle on the ground? His hands and legs were stretched out and two cops were holding him down. Blood was squirting out of his head.

"You got the victim on the ground!" I screamed to the cops.

Suge is looking up at me, and I could see the bleeding getting worse.

"Let him go!" I'm yelling. "He's been shot at!"

They let him up and as soon as they did, Suge and I ran to the BMW to try to get Pac out of the car. The door was stuck for some reason, and I could hear Suge saying over and over again, "I know how to open it. I know how to open it."

I reached for Pac through the window. The medallion and his jersey were soaked in blood and his body was trembling, like he was cold. Through tears, I started talking to him, "You're gonna be okay. You're gonna be okay."

By the time Suge got the door open, the police and the ambulance had arrived, and we got him on the ground.

I knelt down next to him and touched him, "You're gonna be okay, Pac." I was trying to keep him conscious. "Pac, you're okay, you're okay." As I'm kneeling down beside him, I could see him looking up at me. "Frank, I can't breathe," he whispered. "I can't breathe."

"No man, you're okay," I cried.

But he kept repeating it over and over again. "I can't breathe. I can't breathe."

With his own strength, I watched him move both of his hands and cross them over his body. With his eyes open, he took a deep breath and let out a sigh. He closed his eyes.

That was the last time I saw him breathe on his own.

CHAPTER EIGHTEEN

SCAPEGOAT

"You ever feel like your luck's running out, man? Lately, I feel like my luck's been running out."
—*Spoon to Stretch, in* Gridlock'd

I flew home to California on September 11 on America West, to pick up some clothes. I'd only planned to be in Las Vegas overnight, but I'd been by Pac's bedside since the shooting occurred. As I got on the plane to return to Las Vegas, all I could think about was Pac lying up in that hospital bed, and I'm hoping and wishing and praying he's getting better.

I sat in my seat, staring at my ticket blankly, and I notice it says gate number 6. And the 6 is circled. Then I look at my seat number, and it's seat 13, and that's circled. I notice the flight number, and realize it's flight 66, which is listed right by the gate number. I've got a 666, the death sign of the devil, and a 13, an unlucky number, on my ticket. I looked at the numbers I was dealt and that's when I started praying to God, that I make it back to Vegas and that the flight lands.

I'm generally not a superstitious person, but too much had hit me over the past week and I was feeling all wrong about everything. I'm picturing my boy up in there, with a long-ass scar slicing Thug Life in half, and it was all too much to handle.

I landed, but I still didn't feel steady.

I drove to my aunt's house. She lives in Las Vegas, and we had plans to have dinner that night. Along the way, I see Hammer drive by my car, and he waved. He's in his Hummer and he rolled down the window and asks if I'm on the way to the hospital. I told him I was going to get something to eat, and that I would be at the hospital in the morning.

Around midnight, I got a page from Reggie. It didn't take long before the numbers I was dealt on the plane to start tossing some shit luck my way. Hammer apparently went straight to the hospital and proceeded to tell everybody I'm driving around the Strip with some white girl in my car. I don't know where he got that idea, but I was alone and I certainly wasn't out for a joyride.

Anyway, Reggie says Suge wants to see me right away. I told him I'd be there in a half an hour. I pulled up to the mansion, and the guard let me through. Reggie answered the door, and told me Suge's back in his red room, the master bedroom.

It never looked ominous to me before that night, but I didn't like the looks of it now.

Suge gets up and walks out to the pool area, with me following him. In the dark night, the pool cast an eerie shadow over everything. I realized for the first time Suge's house had all the gangsta trappings. He'd seen *Scarface* one time too many, and so had I.

Needless to say, the place was quiet, wasn't nothing going on that night.

We sat down outside and it was me, Suge, and Reggie.

"You know they gonna wanna talk to you tomorrow," he said to me. "The detectives."

"Okay," I said.

"I need you to go along with the story, that the chain was snatched. That you and Pac went in to the MGM Grand, and after the fight, y'all seen the nigga that snatched the chain."

I tell him, alright, whatever. It wouldn't change anything, and the story he was asking me tell was a modified version of what actually happened at the Lakewood Mall, with only the date and the players changed.

Both Suge and Reggie thought the detectives were going to contact me the next day, Friday the thirteenth. They didn't.

I left Suge's house and headed back to the Luxor for a restless sleep. All I was seeing was black.

I got to the hospital at eight A.M., and as I pulled up to park, a van pulled up in front of me and out came Tupac's mother and aunt.

For some reason, Reggie had told me to stay clear of the family. When he told me, I didn't understand why. He said it was because they were upset with me. As I look back now, I wonder if that wasn't the beginning of what seemed to me to be Reggie covering his own ass.

We got to the hospital at the same time and I walked in with them and held the door for them. Every time I got to the hospital, the first thing I did was check on Pac.

My chair was right outside the door. When I looked at him this morning, he was still laying there, with all the life-support tubes all over him, running through his hand, and his arm, up his nose. His eyes were still closed, but he was breathing with the aid of the life-support machinery.

I went back to my chair to begin my shift of guarding Tupac, and his mom walks down the hall. I gave her a hug, and she hugged me back. I loved Pac's mom, she's always been cool with me, and I didn't understand why I was supposed to steer clear of her. After spending some time in Tupac's room, she came out and sat down beside me. She had tears in her eyes, and I looked at her. I'd wanted to say something to her from the beginning and never did.

Today, I had to say something. I turned to her and said, "Momma Shakur, is everything okay?"

"Yes, Frank," she said, her eyes still wet with tears. She put her hand on my hand, and said, "It'll be okay."

A doctor came out and asked Afeni to step into an adjacent room. I could see them but I couldn't hear what they were saying. He was giving her an update on Pac's condition, and I could sense something was wrong. Two days earlier, I'd asked the head surgeon what Pac's condition was, how serious it was, and how many times he was shot. He told me he was shot twice, and sustained two injuries. His hand, which was on his leg, took a bullet that went through the hand, through his leg, hit a thigh bone, and lodged up into his chest. That was the first bullet. The second came through his right side, and that's the one that ruptured his lung and some of his intestines. The doctor only removed one bullet, the one that went into his lung. He couldn't remove the one in his chest, because Pac was too weak. Depending on his recovery, however, he would be able to remove it eventually. I asked him what his recovery potential was and he told me Pac had a 50-50 chance. This was on September 11.

It made me feel hopeful and the doctor reassured me, "He's strong. He's trying to hold on."

*   *   *

The first day I went to look in on him, though, I lost it. I walked in the room and he was lying there, bloated with all the fluids they were pumping into him. His eyes were closed but they were pussy yellow. Pus was just running out of them. You couldn't see his eyes, just a yellow film of thick puss. I wasn't prepared to see him in this condition. He was completely naked. The only area covered was his genitals.

The following day, his eyes went back to normal, but they were still closed and you couldn't see them.

Every day, I sat beside him and held his hand and talked to him.

"I'm sorry, Pac," I told him. "I know if you wake up you're going to be very mad, I don't know what you would say to me or what would happen, but I don't care, as long as you wake up. I need you to get better."

I prayed and talked to him every day I was there. It wasn't easy being there.

Every day at the hospital, I took a lot of shit, but I handled it. I still showed up for work and had to look at all these angry faces, deal with the whispering and the finger-pointing. I just dealt with it, I've never been one to run and hide, and why should I start now? The actress Jasmine Guy was there, and she was cool. I spoke with her for a while, I'd met her before on the video shoot of "Two of America's Most Wanted." She was sad, like we all were.

I was so buried in my own grief I wasn't thinking about taking the looks I was getting seriously. Other security guards, however, were. They started warning me to watch my back and be careful. They told me not to be driving around by myself, and to check my room, and all this kind of shit. They were looking out for me, and I even sensed some of them were actually focusing their attention on me, like, it was me they were protecting.

Yaasmyn called in the Black Panthers. At the time of his death, she was running his Euphanasia office for him. She and Pac got into it a lot. He threatened to fire her a few times, he was screaming at the top of his lungs at her one night in the trailer, while Pac was shooting *Gridlock'd*. He felt shit wasn't getting done around the office, and it was frustrating him. He never fired her, it was just heated talk, but despite the fact she knew how Pac was, she was acting like I was the bad guy.

The fucked thing was, before this, I had a really close relationship

with Yaasmyn. She knew I was on top of my job and she'd praised me for
it. Every time I had to be anywhere or pick him up for something, I was
on time or early, and this impressed her. When he would take off before
I arrived somewhere, I'd call her up and ask what was up? She'd say,
"Yeah, Frank baby, I know you supposed to meet him, but you know Pac.
He's got a mind of his own, he's impatient."

The attitude was always, So what? You're getting paid. It's your job,
so just go home.

Not anymore it wasn't.

What else could I do? I just took it like a man.

In the car with me that night was Yak—Yaasmyn's son—Malcolm and
Kay. They know what happened. Malcolm and I talked about it right after
the shooting, and they already knew the issue of the gun. They never
tripped about it. Malcolm was the oldest out of all them, he was twenty-
one. He realized none of us did anything, or could have done anything.

I remember driving to the hospital after the shooting, and saying to
him, "Fuck, man, this is a bad situation."

"You know what, man, we all gotta clear our heads," he said. "We
gotta think about what happened, and then figure it out. Someone knows
who did it, someone's gonna be out bragging about it, and we gonna find
out."

"Man," I told him, "I don't know what happened any more than you
do. We were all caught off guard."

Malcolm had been sitting behind Yak, on the passenger side of the
car in the back, and he was staring out the window directly at the white
Cadillac. Yak was looking straight ahead. Malcolm was thinking about the
gas, wondering if we were going to run out or not. He saw the car rolling
by, he actually saw the shooter, and by the time he realized what had just
gone down, the shooter had already sped away. It was like a spaceship
had beamed down, snatched him, and took him away, it was that fast.

For her part, Yaasmyn didn't give a fuck. One day at the hospital, she
came up to me and said, "Frank, why is that multimillion-dollar baby lying
up in there? What happened?"

I told her. She said it didn't make sense that I couldn't go get my gun,
and I told her when Pac's ready to go, Pac's ready to go. You can't stop
him. She knew it was the truth, but she didn't want to hear it. She knew

I'd asked Reggie and Suge, time and time again, to get more security on Pac.

Man, no one was listening, least of all Yaasmyn. The horrible thing is, she's now lost her own boy, Yak, one of the Outlaws. Yak was murdered in New Jersey apartment building a few months after Tupac was shot; he was blasted in a supposed drug deal gone bad. He was only eighteen years old.

All I know is, I was feeling bad enough, without her throwing the blame at me, too. She told me she didn't trust security anymore and they'd called in the Black Panthers to come to the hospital. When she asked where Kevin Hackie, my replacement guard for Pac, was on the night of the shooting, I told her Kevin was in a fight with Reggie over money and decided not to come to Vegas.

Fucking Reggie. Before I spoke with Afeni on the thirteenth, I asked Yaasmyn if I could speak with her, and she told me no, not right now. I respected her decision, and decided I wouldn't approach her, I'd let her approach me.

Everything was getting so crazy. There were hundreds of people outside the hospital each morning when I got to work, and they were all trying to get up to see Pac. Apparently, the *National Enquirer* had circulated the word throughout the hospital that they'd pay $150,000 for a Polaroid picture of Pac lying in that bed. You can rest assured, I wasn't going to let it happen. Fuck that, I wouldn't even think about some shit like that. People were trying, though. They had nurses coming down in there, who weren't supposed to be there. Orderlies were trying to get in, fuckin' janitors, you name it. At first I was thinking these people were just doing their job. When I heard about the *Enquirer* bullshit, though, I realized some of these fools were doing too much of their job, so then we started keeping a real close eye on them. I'm proud of the fact that as far as I know, no picture of Pac exists from that hospital. I didn't want the brotha going out like that.

I watched Afeni leave the empty hospital room after talking to the doctor, and that eerie feeling got worse. It was September 13, not surprisingly, Friday the thirteenth. Ever since the omen on the plane, I couldn't shake the way I was feeling.

When I left the hospital in the afternoon and began the drive back to the hotel, my pager started blowing up. There must've been about fifty pages or more, I couldn't even check them as fast as they were coming in. It was Reggie and Larry paging me, Reggie was paging me to his cell phone, pager and Suge's house, while Larry was paging me back to California.

I got to my room and began returning the pages. The first call I made was to Reggie, and he said, "Get to Suge's house, *now*."

I also called Larry. He told me to watch my back.

I drove to Suge's house, and Reggie met me outside the driveway. He stepped to me and said, "You're gonna catch a lot of heat right now. Just sit there and take it. Everybody's real mad Pac's not doing too good."

All I care about is Pac, and when I heard "he's not doing good," I was ready to lose it.

Then Reggie drops this bomb on me.

"They say you identified yourself as a Marine."

"*What!*"

"Yeah, someone heard you tell the cops after the shooting you were an ex-Marine."

"Reggie, why would I tell somebody I was an ex-Marine?"

"I don't know, bro, but that's what they're saying about you."

He told me to park the car and he was going to walk in with me.

I parked the car near the edge of the driveway so I could get out of there fast.

I quickly recalled the events of that night in my head. There was this punk-ass lieutenant, who tried to tell me my facts were wrong, even though he hadn't witnessed the shooting. Then Detective Brent Becker took my statement and the statements from the Outlaws about what we'd seen, and that was the last conversation I'd had with a cop at the scene. The only other time I spoke with Detective Becker was when he came to see me at the hospital. He asked if anything had changed since I first gave my statement, and I told him no. Nothing about my background in the Marines ever came up. What the fuck was up?

I walked inside and went through the hallway, out through the kitchen and onto the patio, where Suge was sitting at the left end of the table. There's an empty chair to the right of him, and one of his homeboys sat in the middle of the table. Across from him was David Kenner, Death Row's attorney. There was one other guy there, I don't know whether or not he was an attorney or a friend of Suge's, but I heard Suge ask him, "How many tickets did you get?"

"Twelve," he responded.

Suge looked at him and said, "Twelve tickets, twelve muthafuckin' tickets and only four of us went, and only one fuckin' security for Tupac." He was obviously referring to the MGM ticket count.

Suge then turns to me, and says, "What the fuck you gonna do about it? My homeboy's laying up there fighting for his life. And what's this shit about you identifying yourself as a muthafuckin' Marine?"

I said to him, "Suge, I didn't identify myself as a Marine."

His homeboy jumped in and said, "Yes you did. That's what the police said."

"I don't care what the police said. I didn't."

The homeboy didn't respond, but Suge snapped: "You a liar; I heard you!"

I looked directly at him and said, "Suge, you didn't hear me. When I came into the police line, I was the only one they let in. You were laying on the ground, with blood gushing out of your head. I ran over there, told them who I was, and who you were, and that's when they let you up off the ground. That's when you and I ran around to the car."

He didn't say nothing about that. He was still determined to believe I said some shit about being a Marine, which had nothing to do with anything, but I'm beginning to see the smear come down heavy.

Suddenly, the telephone rings and it's Calvin Tubbs, who's helping to run Death Row. He was calling from the hospital every few minutes to give Suge an update on Pac.

Suge listened into the receiver, said, "Alright," then hung up the phone.

He began screaming at me, "*I still don't understand why you didn't have your fuckin' gun!*"

I said, "Suge, I already told you on Sunday, the day after the shooting. Remember, I came to the house, we sat in your office, and we talked for about an hour or so, going over the details. You didn't say anything about it then, after I explained all this to you."

I can look back now and see he was pissed off about Pac's update and wasn't thinking rationally, but it still fucked with me. We'd already had a meeting the day after the shooting. I went over the whole day, from when the attorney told us to leave our guns in the hotel or in our car to when Pac, at the last minute, threw me Kidada's keys and asked to drive the Li'l Homies.

When I repeated the story, I saw Suge look at Reggie, and Reggie look at Suge and they both started shaking their heads. I fuckin' saw it coming like a ton of bricks. I was taking the fall, and there was nothing I could do about it.

I thought to myself, *Oh shit, this whole fuckin' deck is stacked against me.* That's when I started defending myself, because I'm not the kind of nigga who's gonna take it lying down. I told him Tupac had two bodyguards with him that whole entire day, and when he asked me what happened to Michael Moore, why wasn't he with us, I told him, he'd gotten a phone call from Al Gittens, who Reggie had made a security supervisor, asking him to come to 662 because he was needed there. "I have no control over who's going where. I'm one person. I've asked for extra security for Pac time and time again."

That's when he looked at me and said, "You're right, Frank. So what happened?"

I looked him dead in the eye and said, "Suge, it's not my security company."

Suge paused for a moment and turned to Reggie.

"So what happened, Reg? How come Tupac didn't have two or three security guards? He's the most fuckin' important artist on this record label and he's walking around with one bodyguard."

Reggie explained something about having meetings with me and Suge on the subject and how nothing ever came about after the meetings.

I looked at that muthafucka and wanted to rip his throat out. My friend was dying. The whole time I'm getting heat, being one bodyguard, when there should have been two or three guards with him at all times.

I don't know if there was a ticket problem or not, but all I know is, me, Pac, Suge, and his homeboy went into the fight. Twenty security guards were at 662, waiting on us to get there after the fight.

No one said anything at this point, and I remember thinking that David Kenner'd been awfully quiet for a while. Wonder what role he's gonna play in this.

Suddenly Suge says to me, "Bet you got your fuckin' gun on you now."

I said, "No I don't, Suge. It's in the car."

Then he walks up on me, and I'm thinking, *Oh shit*, because he's standing up. This is the first time Suge's ever given me any of this shit before. I'm looking at this brotha, who's always shown me love, flexing up on me, and I wasn't prepared for this at all.

Reggie pipes in, "Suge, it's in his car. I saw it in his car."

Then the phone rings, Suge answers and listens. He doesn't speak. He took the phone and threw it across the table.

"It's too fuckin' late now. Can't nobody do nothin' for him. He's gone." His voice was cracking. He stands up, and just walks away.

When he walked away, everybody at the table stood up. I just sat there, and I started crying.

Then I looked at Reggie, and said, "You're fucked. You fucked me over. You didn't stand up for me, you just let this whole fuckin' thing come down on me like this. You let me take the fuckin' heat. Why didn't you stand up for me?"

He said, "Bro, you know, I couldn't. You just have to take it."

"That's bullshit. I'm getting blamed for Tupac's death by Suge, by his family, everybody's pointing the finger at me. It ain't right, it ain't right."

I'm still crying through my words, and we're standing beside that bloodred pool and for the first time, it's hitting. *It's over. This whole thing is over. Pac's dead and I'm fucked.*

Right then, Reggie said, "Just go, go, go. Get out of here. Get your shit out of the hotel and leave, go home."

I start freaking out. He walks me out of the back gate to the driveway. My car's blocked in but I manage to get it out. Tears are still streaming down my face, and I looked at that muthafucka and said, "This is fucked-up, Reggie." For the first time, I'm scared now. I started to shake, and as I'm pulling out of there, I started calling people. I called Larry, and I called Michael and my partner K. J. I'm driving and just dialing, calling muthafuckas because I'm upset. I told them what happened, because I wanted them to be witness if anything happened to me. They were all back in California and I needed them to know what went down.

Everybody said the same thing. Get the fuck out of there. Michael told me to just leave my car at my aunt's, fly home, and he'd pick me up from the airport.

I told him, "I'm gonna drive my fuckin' car."

I told him I was gonna leave late.

I went back to the Luxor, grabbed all my shit and checked in to a different hotel. I just sat there, and I was trippin'—I'm nervous, frightened and upset. I was told not to go to the hospital, and I can't even say goodbye to my boy. The shit was so fucked-up.

I got on the road about eleven o'clock at night. My cell phone rang, and it was Reggie. He told me, "Suge wanna talk to you. He's gonna call you."

It's now about midnight, and I wait for the call.

The phone rings. It's Suge.

"Sorry about earlier today," he said. "We're all upset. I know that Pac loved you, and you loved him. I don't think, by no means, you had anything to do with anything. We were all just upset."

He paused, and then added, "I have nothing but love for you."

What the fuck, I didn't know what to say or think.

He continued. "We're gonna take the boat out on a lake tomorrow—get your girl and why don't you join us?"

I told him I was almost home and I'd have to take a raincheck.

That was the last time I ever spoke with Suge Knight.

I spent the next two days in a stony haze, thinking about everything that went down and trying to make some sense of it. I listened to his music and looked at the pictures above my mantelpiece, and I was so depressed. I'm thinking, *What the fuck.* On September 16, I went to a tattoo parlor and got a tattoo on my shoulder, it says, "In Memory of Tupac, Only God Can Judge You, Revelation 20: 12."

I learned later, everyone from Death Row had gone out and done the same. I was the first one, then Suge, the Li'l Homies, and other friends of his. It was a trip that we'd all had the same idea. I guess it's like pouring out a little liquor over the grave, a mourning ritual.

I don't know what their reasoning was, but for me, I wanted to keep a memory of him in my heart, and now, he's always gonna be there.

CHAPTER NINETEEN

ME AGAINST THE WORLD

If you believe in angels, then you'll understand me when I tell you I believe I have an angel watching over me. I think back to that day in Las Vegas when Suge was punking me at his house in Las Vegas, and I don't know what would've happened to me if that phone call hadn't come through. I'll never know, because right as things were getting to the point of no return, Suge got the call from the hospital, telling him Tupac was dead. I believe that call, telling Suge about Pac's death, might possibly have saved my life. Who knows how far things would've gotten? If you think about it, given the situation, it might even have been Pac intervening from the Other Side.

After the day, I never saw Suge Knight again, except on the news. Although Reggie told Suge I wasn't working for Wrightway anymore, I stayed on throughout the month of October. Reggie gave me a new detail, working twelve-hour shifts at a closed-down church in Inglewood he had a contract with. I heard he told Suge he'd fired me, but the truth is, I was in some sort of living purgatory. I did absolutely nothing all day, I just sat there for the entire twelve hours. Every now and then, one of the other security guards would come up early to spend time talking with me.

The detail ended, and more time went by, and eventually the phone had stopped ringing. Wrightway was no longer calling me to give me work, and I pretty much figured it was over. The silence was hard for me to take, because my life had been so hectic before the shooting. In my own mind, I was struggling to move on with or without the help of Death Row.

Shortly after the detail ended, Suge was sent to prison on a parole violation, and suddenly my phone started ringing. Suge had taken heat over his participation in the MGM scuffle, and lo and behold, who did they turn to now? They decided I was their one credible witness. I was valuable to them again. I never understood why they decided to come to me to be a witness. The only thing I could figure is, they expected me to lie for Suge Knight. I wasn't about to perjure myself on the witness stand. The videotape already showed him in the middle of the fight, getting his kicks in. If he wanted me to say something about the necklace being snatched off Pac's neck, he had come to the wrong guy. I wouldn't do that in that court. I was willing to tell the detectives his story initially, to go along with what Death Row was saying. That's before it was going to have an impact on the situation one way or the other. Now that I would be asked to do this in front of a judge, I wasn't going to do anything but tell the truth.

I began keeping a tape recorder next to the phone. I recorded dozens and dozens of conversations, with Reggie, Death Row attorneys David Kenner and Milton Grimes, Detective Brent Becker from Las Vegas, as well as other members of security.

My testimony would have hurt Suge more than helped him. I explained all this to David Kenner. In the meantime, Death Row found me to be a very useful person again, and they constantly called me. They wanted me to look at the video the MGM supplied them with. Once I finally agreed to look at the video, they subpoenaed me to go to court the next day to Suge's hearing.

I went with the mind-set I was either going to plead the Fifth Amendment or tell the truth. I was tossing and turning all night, trying to figure out what to do. It was do or die. I had to make a decision, and I chose to watch my own back this time out. I had to look out for myself, because if not, I'd be looking out for people who'd already turned their back on me once. By this I mean, I knew I'd be helping Suge more by staying out of the mix than if I testified for him. Although this was also in my best interest, I also believed it was a way of, ironically, keeping my loyalty and respect with Suge. They didn't see it this way, and the pressure was on.

Each court date they had, my name came up. They started throwing my name around, detectives were calling me, and it continued to get stranger. The prosecutors began calling me. They wanted me to testify *against* Suge.

I got a phone call from the investigating officer for the D.A.'s office, and they asked me to come down that day. I told them I couldn't make it.

Then for some reason I called Reggie and told him what went down. I guess my old loyalties are hard to break.

The day I got subpoenaed, I went to the courthouse. I sat in the hallway and never got called.

As the trial continued, I was still an important witness in their minds, and after a few weeks passed from the day I called Reggie, the Death Row attorneys began calling again, asking for my cooperation. I told Milton Grimes to go back to Suge and explain to him why I'd taken the position I was taking. I don't know how Suge felt about the news—till this day I don't know.

I'm a true believer in things happening for a reason, and as difficult as it was to watch the Death Row family turn its back on me, I realized, again, perhaps it was meant to be. Had they remained down with me in my time of need, I might have helped Suge out in his time of need. My loyalty might have been so strong, I would have done whatever I could have to help my boss. Since they weren't there for me, I saw their true colors when they were backed into a corner, and I didn't like what I saw. It wasn't the strength of character found in a man like Tupac and a man like myself.

They turned their backs on me, and it was time to turn my back on them and begin a new chapter in my life.

"They want you dead."

"What do you mean, they want me dead? Who wants me dead?"

"D. R."

I couldn't believe what I was hearing. It was my homeboy, Larry, who worked for Reggie. He'd heard some shit around the office.

There was a long pause on the other end of the phone before Larry let out a sigh.

"Yeah," he said slowly. "They said you told a lot of stuff against Suge, and Pac. They said they got a police report, and it says you said that Suge, Buntree, and Pac were beating the guy up . . . Look, I don't know what to tell you but the rumor's out. They don't want you around."

"Are you sure about that?" I asked.

"Look Frank, I quit . . . They don't trust me anymore. They know you're like my brother. Regardless, you're my brother. Even if we don't see each other for another thirty years, we'll always be tight."

I hung up the phone. *Stay cool,* I told myself. I had no idea whether any of it was true. *Muthafuck.* Regardless of everything that had gone down, I couldn't believe Suge or anyone else was gonna pull this type of punk shit. If the threats were real, I didn't know for a fact they were coming from Suge.

I remember Kevin Hackie telling me I had too trusting of a heart. I didn't want to believe Suge could be playing me like this. Shit, before the shooting, he'd always been cool with me. I remembered the night we were eating at Monty's in Beverly Hills. That was the first time he saw I drove a Mercedes, 500SL—he had one just like it.

"All you need is some custom rims, Frank," he said. "Call my office tomorrow, and I'll hook you up." Eventually, Suge gave me $8,000 worth of Antera rims for my car. I didn't have any beef with this man. Besides it was *his* fight. He was the one who jumped in to beat on Orlando Anderson that night at the MGM Grand after the Tyson bout. My only involvement was to try to quash it, to get them out of there safely.

The fucked thing was, Larry was a reliable source.

I decided to check another source, in the back of my mind, I assumed Reggie would know what was going on, and Michael Moore was the closest security guard to Reggie. I located Michael's phone number, dialed, and he answered. Ever since the shooting, I'd avoided Michael because I knew he was real tight with Reggie. I knew Michael cared about me, too, and I didn't want to put him in the middle of this shit.

I told him why I was calling.

"Michael, Larry said Death Row wants me dead."

The line was silent.

I repeated it. "That's what I just heard. I just got a phone call saying Death Row wants me dead."

Silence.

Dammit, I thought, *it's true.*

Finally, I heard him say, "Okay. I wasn't gonna tell you this . . . but that's affirmative. That's true."

Another pause. This time, I'm at a loss for words.

"How can I say this? That rumor is out there, you know what I'm saying? That rumor is out there. From the people that I talked to, they're taking it personal."

"How serious are they?" I heard him ask rhetorically, before answering his own question: "Put it this way, if Suge don't get out, you're gonna be in deep trouble, Frank."

"I have nothing to do with Suge being in jail!" I said.

"I know that. You know that. But you're not playing ball, Frank. It would look better if you played ball."

So that's what this was about. I had refused to perjure myself on the witness stand, I refused to risk going to jail for Death Row, to take the heat for their bullshit.

"If I were you, I'd think about your family, Frank."

Michael was still talking, but by now I'd slipped deep into my head. I realized they were blaming me for everything—*everything*. I started getting angry. Is this how you do a family member . . . a brotha? You kick him to the side. You disown him. You unemploy him. What did I do to deserve that?

It's funny, though, because they kept flipping the script. Suge goes to jail on a probation hearing, and all of a sudden, I'm a brotha again. They need me to testify, tell a few lies, "play ball." It's none of my business I tell them, and the next thing I know, I'm getting death threats.

Well, I wasn't gonna run and hide. I decided to make one more phone call, this time to David Kenner, Death Row's longtime attorney. We didn't beat around the bush. Kenner pulled out Detective Brent Becker's report.

If you recall, Becker was with Las Vegas Metro and he rang me up in early October, before everything started going down with Suge. He told me he was calling at David Kenner's urging; apparently Kenner told him my memory had been jogged and I remembered some other events. He'd caught me off guard, but I recalled the meeting I had with Suge the day before Pac died. I told Becker Suge's story. I would never have told Becker that story if I'd known there was more drama to come. I thought it had ended with Pac's death and this was just a footnote Death Row wanted added to the story. At the time Becker had called, Suge was still running Death Row.

By the time I called David Kenner, the tide had turned. Kenner began reading me Becker's report. I couldn't believe what I was hearing. Kenner was reading one lie after another. Not the lie about the chain, but an entire report filled with things I did not say. It said I named names of those involved in the fight at the MGM. It said I gave the police their gang affiliations. I don't even know the real names of Suge's homeboys, nor would I give two shits about their gang affiliations. He kept reading me lies.

"Stop right there, Mr. Kenner. I did not say that," I said. "I will testify that the police report you are reading has been falsified." My heart was thumping loudly. It appeared someone had lied, and I was the one getting death threats.

Kenner continued to read the report.

"Mr. Kenner," I interrupted again. "I will testify that those statements are incorrect. I did not say that . . . I wish you would call anybody who has any concern about this and tell them what I'm telling you. I've been getting death threats. I've been told I'd better not step in court. That's why I called you today, because I have nothing to hide. I had nothing against Suge."

We hung up the phone. I had this sinking feeling. I didn't understand what was happening.

I was interviewed again by the Las Vegas detectives in March 1997, after the *L.A. Times* ran a piece about how no one from the Las Vegas Metro Police had contacted me or Malcolm to see if we could identify the shooter. Apparently, they had some suspects in custody, but we were never called to see if we could ID them. They came to L.A. with some photos for me to look at, but I couldn't for certain identify anyone from the pictures. At this time, they told me David Kenner had called them in October and repeated the conversation I had with him.

I let everybody know about the death threats—my attorney, Suge's attorneys, the detectives, the newspapers—and I'm sure everything got back to Suge. Did he really want me dead? I didn't take the threats lightly, but I didn't change my lifestyle. I didn't stop going to the places I went to, but I was careful. Again, I dealt with it. Again I realized I was in this alone.

The irony of everything is, here I am, one of the only eyewitnesses they have to the events of that evening who hasn't turned up dead. The other key witness, Yak, had already been murdered.

All eyes on me, I think to myself. *I'm all they've got left.*

I keep hearing Tupac's words in my sleep, *"My only fear of death is reincarnation."*

Tupac my brotha, you were right. You're in a better place.

*   *   *

As I watch all the shit come down on Death Row right now, and all the lawsuits that everyone's now embroiled in, I think to myself, Pac would be turning over in his grave. He was always so straight-up about shit, and didn't like people who were false. His mom is suing Death Row and his dad is suing his mother—which is pretty unfortunate because he wasn't part of Pac's young life, and now he wants to be part of the inheritance. All you have to do is listen to track 15 on *Strictly 4 My Niggaz.* The song is called "Papa'z Song," and it's dedicated to the dad who was never there for him, who didn't give a shit. *"Had to play catch by myself,"* is one memorable line. My guess is, Pac would've never even heard from his father if he hadn't made it over.

It's fucked-up, because if he was still alive, I tell you this, no one would be trying to pull shit with him, because they feared him. Now that he's not here to defend himself, they're crawling out of the woodwork trying to get their piece of him.

I did have a true friendship with him and the people close to him, and it hurts me nobody called me to see how I was taking it. No one thought about my feelings or what I had seen or had gone through. I'd never watched anybody die before, and had never been blamed for someone's death.

Death Row had always been so proud of its status as a family. They treated their employees like family and always told us, "We're a family. If shit goes down, we take care of our own."

When the shit went down, I saw how they took care of their own. They threw him out to the wolves, and that's what happened to me. Till this day, I don't know if any questions came down on Reggie from Suge. They were tighter than brothers, they'd grown up together since they were little kids, and loyalty's a son of a bitch. Whatever happened behind closed doors between Reggie and Suge, I can't say one way or another. All I know is Reggie would know enough to shut up and keep his mouth shut and just take whatever Suge gave him.

I will say this about the aftermath, though. Every one of the security guards came up to me before they left Las Vegas and told me it wasn't my fault. They didn't want me to take the responsibility on my shoulders.

I don't care who would have been there, none of us could have done shit. If somebody rolls up and they're shooting, you ain't got time to respond. If I'd been in the car, I would've been shot. They all knew what was up, and they all showed concern for me. Michael Moore and Leslie were the only two who defended me to Suge and Reggie.

"When something goes wrong, they look for a scapegoat," says Michael. "Frank just happened to be the goat who was there. They had to blame somebody. But it could have been any of us. The same thing would have happened to me. There would have been no change. I would have been thrown the keys, and I would have gotten in the car without my gun. And I would have taken the fall. It was fate, and it wasn't Frank's fault. The fact Tupac was also a friend to Frank, means he takes a couple hits."

Leslie broke it down to Suge in legal terms, explaining how it would have been illegal for me to shoot back. Suge didn't know what he meant, so he spelled it out.

" 'They rolled up on you guys, put guns out the car and shot, then took off burning rubber. Correct?' I asked him," says Les. "He nodded, and I told him by the time Frank would've gotten out of the car, unholstered the weapon and fired, he would've been firing at fleeing felons, and he would've gotten in trouble. Police officers cannot shoot in Nevada at fleeing felons. He didn't want to hear that. Suge wanted me to validate what everybody else agreed on, which was Frank should have shot back."

There was a consensus among the other guards that if there had been ten of us traveling with Pac, we still wouldn't have been able to react before the car sped away. It all went down in seconds. If you compare it to the New York incident, where there was a lot of security on hand, no one got the shooter. No one even saw the shooter that day.

When it came time to talk to the detectives, I went alone.

All I know is, during the interview I was forced to relive the incident one more time. In my mind's eye, I see a very slight side profile of the shooter, because when he stuck his hand out the window, a portion of his face came out. I saw the shape of his nose, and the silhouette of his profile. I could identify him as black, because his arm was as black as the gun. He was wearing gloves, as well. (Malcolm, who saw the shooter dead-on, never met with them to try to ID him.)

The one thing I had to explain again, is why I didn't go after the Cadillac. I wasn't about to go chasing the Cadillac with an empty gas tank. Besides, my only concern was for Suge and Pac at that point. I didn't know if they were dead or alive; when the car sped away I realized Suge was alive. When I began following Suge, in my head, I thought someone else would have the sense to follow the car. I'm pretty certain someone did, because shit don't go down like that and nobody not do something about it. I can't say who, but someone must have. There were too many cars there, and a lot of Suge's homeboys were in these cars. They were Compton gangstas and this is what they *do*. This is their reality and they know what to do instantly. I'm sure it was done, and I'm sure they shot back, because the police found some other bullet casings. The police continuously asked me, "Are you sure you didn't have a gun? Are you sure you didn't fire a gun?" In every interview I had, I had to repeat myself. They asked me if I heard anyone else return fire, and I said no. All I heard was the initial shooting. The big question the police wanted answered was, "Who shot back?"

The word circulating around now is the shooting was supposed to have been some planned, orchestrated act. Suge had something to do with it.

I personally don't believe Suge put the hit on Pac. Although plenty of shit was off that day, from the lack of security to the lack of preparations—I couldn't carry a gun; I didn't have a phone; it was Suge's homeboy who got Pac into the fight at the MGM; Suge himself had time to make a phone call before we left the hotel—I still find it too hard to believe. Even if he didn't put a direct hit on Pac, a lot of people feel Death Row did nothing to try to slow that boy down. They believe Suge Knight fueled Pac's flames.

The fact is, no one could tell Pac what to do so I don't know if I can even pin that on Suge. Also, I saw him with my own two eyes after the shooting and Suge was grieving. Not to mention logic will tell you, a man that big wouldn't have invited a hail of bullets in his car. Common sense says Suge's a bigger target than Tupac, and those bullets were flying throughout the car. Clearly it wasn't his time to go. It's true, he and Pac were starting to have problems, and I've heard all the rumors about Suge taking out a $52 million life-insurance policy on Pac, and standing as the sole beneficiary. But I don't know how much Suge knew at that point about Pac's dissatisfaction, and no matter how I look at it, I don't see Suge setting the whole thing up.

Whether or not it was a professional hit, doesn't seem that relevant to me. Serious gangstas can shoot, and the job looked clean. The bullets came into the car in a straight line, *rat-a-tat-tat*, on the side Tupac was sitting on. I know they knew who they were shooting at. Without a doubt, they knew who he was. Whether they cared if they were gonna hit Suge or not, I don't know.

Nevertheless, I felt like it was me against the world. I went from being a hero in New York to being "the brotha who let Tupac get shot." I was the fall guy.

There was a meeting after Pac's shooting I wasn't invited to. All the other guards were there, along with Reggie and Suge and the artists. I found out Michael Moore defended me. He got in trouble for it, too. The point of the meeting was for the artists to bash security. According to Michael, Hammer and Kurupt were going off.

Hammer was a new artist, who didn't like security to begin with—we had problems with him all the time. He fueled the fire and said security was fucked up anyway. We had our trouble with him at Super Bowl XXX in Phoenix. It was at a big hall and there were maybe three or four of us on hand, and we had to look after Suge and Hammer and a couple of Suge's homeboys. Hammer wanted to dictate to us how to do our job. At one point, he stepped to me and told me I needed to be behind Suge, so nobody could come up from behind. I looked at him and said, "Don't tell me how to do my job." Reggie got into it with him, too.

Hammer, from day one, got off on the wrong foot. Why he had the beef, I don't know. But we had a number of problems with Hammer. One time he got into it with Suge because after one of the Tyson fights, he tried to bring forty people into 662. He got caught and it did not go over well.

I never got a chance to meet with the artists to talk about what happened. The only one I heard back from was Snoop. The fact that Kurupt turned against me really hurt. Kurupt loved me to death after New York, and I couldn't believe he was saying shit about me. He had wanted to hire me as his personal bodyguard during the time Tupac wanted me, and of course, Tupac won out because he had seniority.

I couldn't defend myself, and I don't know the details of the conversation but the bulk of the accusations were surrounded by the question of where the gun was.

It was that night that Hammer reported back to everyone that he saw me the next night after the shooting with some girl in my car driving down the Strip. I wondered where the fuck he got that from. I saw him and I waved to him, but I was on my way to the hospital. He told everybody I was out partying and in a festive mood.

Whatever. Can't change it now, but sure know who my friends are.

CHAPTER TWENTY

DEATH IN LOS ANGELES: THE SHOOTING OF BIGGIE SMALLS

Everyone knows cops shouldn't just aimlessly start shooting. If they do, we read about in the morning paper. No matter how many times an innocent bystander's been shot or wounded in the past year by a licensed officer, it's too many.

In my situation, there's no way I would've just started shooting. I would have needed a clean shot of the shooter to begin firing and the Strip was packed with people that night, so there's a good chance a bullet would have landed somewhere it wasn't supposed to; and since I wasn't allowed to be carrying a gun in the state of Nevada that night, I could very well be sitting behind bars. But it's too late to be thinking about "what-if's."

No matter what really went down, look at the situation with Biggie and tell me something could have been done. Biggie had two people with him, Li'l Caesar and his bodyguard, who was a Compton Crip.

The other day I was in a barbershop and the barber was from New York, and we were talking, and he started to say he'd heard some rumor that the guy who shot Biggie was his former bodyguard and it was over a debt. The dude said Biggie owed him money and he warned Biggie not to come to the West Coast. Biggie not only came to the West Coast after being warned not to, he went over to a South Side Crips park and hung out there for a half a day. The guy showed up and he told Biggie he'd better pay up. I guess nothing happened because Biggie showed up later at the Soul Train Awards, and ended up at the *Vibe* postshow party which he attended before he got shot.

I've heard two separate accounts of what happened that night. The first story suggests it was a drive-up, identical to what went down with Tupac. The driver pulls up in a black Jeep and opens fire on the side of the car. The second story says the shooter came up off a street corner, and when Biggie pulled up to a stoplight, he stepped to the car and shot into it. It's still unclear to me which one really occurred but needless to say, as much as people seem to want the shooting to be part of an East Coast–West Coast conspiracy, the facts point to a beef Biggie had with a guy who felt he'd been ripped off, and he took him out. It wasn't right but it happened. If it's true, and the guy had threatened Biggie, then he'd look pretty fuckin' stupid if he didn't follow through with his threat. You have to remember, this shit is serious. No one's joking about gangstas on the West Coast. People get murdered all the time over beefs, and if Biggie's hanging out with the bad boys, he can't just walk away when it gets too deep. These dudes don't care if he's famous, to them, it's another day at the office.

Not to mention since Tupac's death, Puffy and Biggie have come out on the West Coast as if they live here, and they have an open range of coming out here without any fear. Tupac's dead and Suge's in prison, so that right there always made me think there was someone who—just out of love for Tupac, someone who wouldn't shed a tear over Biggie's death—may have had his hand in it. That doesn't make it an East Coast–West Coast beef, it makes it personal. Those were my initial feelings on the shooting of Biggie, and when the news came out later, that it was his former bodyguard and it happened over money—even if that's the case, it doesn't mean it didn't have something to do with gangstas not liking how Puffy and Biggie were cozying up to the West.

I was watching *Yo! MTV Raps* and I saw Daz and Snoop in New York taping the show, and I was like, *What the fuck!* Pac must be turning over in his grave. My first instincts were, *Why is Snoop in New York, not wearing his Death Row chain, when we had all that drama back there?*

It just seemed all wrong. I thought, *Damn, the brotha's selling out.* Then they introduced the "New York, New York" video and Snoop talked about the drama that went down when that video was shot, but said, "Now, it's all good, because we're all one now." I wondered what was going on. Then I heard about the peace treaty Snoop had with Puffy on the *Steve Harvey Show* and I really couldn't figure it out. The next thing that happens, is, Biggie gets killed. So then I said, *Ah-hah! That's what them muthafuckas get for thinking they had free range of the West Coast.* These were my thoughts, and you can bet there's some truth to this shit because everyone knows if Tupac were alive, Biggie and Puffy wouldn't have been out here, and Snoop and Daz wouldn't have been in New York. Period.

I didn't give Biggie's bodyguard one thought, because his situation was so different from mine. They never mentioned anything about the bodyguard until much later. It appears he was in the backseat, and Li'l Caesar was driving. Why he didn't shoot back, and why he didn't get off any rounds isn't a mystery in his case, because he—keep this in mind—is a South Side Crip. Now if the shooter was a South Side Crip, and the bodyguard's a South Side Crip and they're from the same set, what real reason would this Crip have to get out of the car and shoot back at his homeboy? Why would he take out the shooter? If they're from the same set, chances are they grew up together in the same neighborhood, they know the same people. This is just a job for the guy who's in the backseat, okay? It wasn't the same as me and Tupac. This wasn't down with Biggie. This guy's from California doing a job when Biggie comes into town. When you look at the reality of the situation, it wouldn't have been wise for him to shoot back, because guess what? They'da blasted a cap in his ass so fast for being a traitor. By not shooting back, he probably saved his own life. After learning of Biggie's death, I never once thought, *Hey, I should reach out to this guy, let him know I've been through it.* The situations were completely different.

I do, however, want to share my thoughts on Biggie. All I can say is, here's another brotha who was taken out who was talented. He's another human being, regardless of anything. We are all God's children, I don't give a fuck what color we are, we all bleed the same color, the same blood. We're made up of the same organs. It's just sad when human being takes out another human being. We're not animals, we don't stalk one another and have territorial places where we can go and where we can't go. That's what animals in the jungle do. We're supposed to be civilized people. God gave us brains and abilities to be as creative as we can be. But instead of using those capabilities, too often we are living like animals in a jungle.

The sad truth is, we're a confused species. We're so smart, we can visit Mars and maybe start developing on other planets, but we can't get shit straight here. I feel like we're already at a point where you better know who you are and where you come from, and your prayers better be in order, because when the time comes, it'll be too late. You better be ready now.

I know Tupac was ready.

PART SIX

THE AFTERMATH

CHAPTER TWENTY-ONE

I AIN'T MAD ATCHA: TO SUGE KNIGHT AND THE DEATH ROW FAMILY

I watched Evander Holyfield when he appeared on *Dateline*. A reporter asked him how he felt about Mike Tyson, and Holyfield responded that he loves Mike Tyson. He also said he hopes Mike gets better. The reporter seemed surprised by this, and Holyfield went on to explain that being a Christian means having a loving heart, and he forgave Mike Tyson instantly, while he was still in the ring, even before he'd gotten back to his corner.

I thought about that for a long time. Tyson tried to disfigure Holyfield, he tried to hurt him permanently. His anger so overpowered him, he became a raging bull. Nevertheless, the man on the receiving end of the rage was a bigger, better, man, to forgive him without hesitation.

I looked at that and applied it to my own situation. How can I, after everything I've been through with Death Row, have any animosity toward anyone involved with that family? I had an amazing year with them, and to be able to share the last year of Tupac Shakur's life was an extraordinary experience. So, to use Tupac's words, I ain't mad atcha. I don't hold a grudge toward anyone. What happened, happened.

I want Suge to know I ain't mad at him. When he came down on me, I think it was more out of grief than true anger. I also believe when he was facing jail time, rather than blame himself for the situation he'd gotten himself into, it was easier to blame me.

Whatever, it no longer keeps me up at night. I've come to peace with the events of the last year, and I hope Suge is searching to find his own peace.

People want villains. It seems they can rest easier at night, if they can view the world with a division between good and evil. The world I come from isn't like that. Suge Knight isn't like that. Whatever bad he's supposedly done in his life, he never showed security anything but respect. He was always cool with me, up until that day at the pool when Pac died, and he apologized for it later. My emotions were fucked up, too. I loved Tupac and he knew that. The only thing I can say is, the truth will come to light. And so far, for the future of Death Row, it looks bad.

Forget good and evil, Suge's story is about intelligence and stupidity.

Suge Knight was the most powerful young black businessman in the industry—he had the American dream at his fingertips. He had access to all the things rich white people have access to, and beyond. Unfortunately, he couldn't leave the gangster mentality behind him. He took it everywhere he went, and it's my belief he should have left that shit behind when he made it, but not forgotten where he came from. You can still be a strong brotha *and* a *down* brotha, by helping your family and your community and those who are close to you.

The difference between Chicago gangstas and what I saw happening in L.A. with Death Row is, their whole objective seemed to be about building a reputation. In Chicago, the whole objective is to gain money. The serious gangstas are in the background, making their money, not posing for pictures and starting public fights.

Although I don't believe Death Row began as a gang, it certainly evolved into something similar to one. When Dre and Suge hooked up to create Death Row Records, the objective was to create music. It went from being a musical entity to a "gang."

It became such because the leader himself decided before anyone else to make that statement. By creating an emblem of gold and diamonds, he was creating a symbol for others to see, and to those who have the gang mentality, it signified Bloods. The day Suge Knight came home wearing the chain, it was on. The chain became a gang-emblem sign and wearing it was like throwing up a gang sign in front of a Crip. Today no one would be caught dead wearing a Death Row chain anywhere because of the bounty for them. No one's wearing them out on the streets anymore.

At the last Mother's Day party, Suge gave all the mothers Death Row chains, smaller than the ones the guys used to wear, but still pure gold. These very women have been jumped on; chains have been snatched off their necks; they've been slapped in public. All because of that emblem.

Suge hooked Reggie up to run Wrightway, and he had an excellent crew working for him, who were very tight and very sharp. He hired good people, with good morals and good backgrounds, but he started nickel and diming people. He must have seen how Suge was living, and he saw the money he was making.

Larry says he was writing up invoices for $30,000 and $40,000 every two weeks. "He started getting petty," says Larry. "If someone worked forty hours, he would try to pay him thirty-six. He came up with bullshit reasons, he didn't want to reimburse expenses, and it was always a big conflict with me and him, because regardless, I'm gonna see to it a person has what they've got coming to them. He wasn't like that." That's one thing I don't miss.

Larry hasn't worked for Reggie since all the shit went down with me after Pac's shooting, says "Reggie was throwing Frank under a bus that day. He'd do anything he has to to get his ass out of the hole. Reggie, for one, isn't prepared for the real shit to go down. He never had to want for anything in his life. His parents have always been very good providers. He'd never been in trouble in his life, then he had to go and get involved in some shit just for money."

Larry thinks Reggie's gonna have the hardest time out of them all, and he's not going to want to face that fate. "Suge, and the other people around him, are tougher," he says. "They've been through more. Reggie's not going to be willing to face that hard time, because he's never been there. He's always been on the other side, he's been the one turning the key. I know if anything really goes down, Reggie's gonna turn on him. He's not going to go to jail."

Larry has a point; whenever a crime leader's turned-out, it's always his right-hand man who does the talking. In Suge's case, he's got someone he should be worrying about even more. Every time a gangster bust goes down, I don't care if it's *The Godfather* or John Gotti—who turns him in? Every time, it's his right-hand man. The one that knows everything. All I know is, you reap what you sow.

They tried to do the same with Pac when he was in the hospital in Vegas. The detectives came by there twice a day sometimes, trying to see if Tupac had regained consciousness and could talk. They asked every time they showed up, "Did he wake up?" They figured he might've seen who shot him and would give them a description. Would he have? Of course. There were problems between him and Suge, so of course he would've told them what he knew. Don't think for a second the detectives weren't hoping Pac's shooting was somehow related to Suge.

If you cut the head off a snake, what do you have? A dying body, a viper that's no use to anyone anymore. That's what happened to Death Row when Suge went down. Suge was the viper, they locked him up, now what can he do? He can't even run his company so it starts going down. As long as he was around to take care of it, it was going to be strong and powerful.

It all came to a screeching halt with Suge's incarceration. Although the business is still open, it's probably not for long. Suge's probably going crazy on lockdown, but just like Tyson biting Holyfield's ear, Suge *had* to get into the fight at the MGM Grand, and no one could have reasoned with him. He didn't say to himself, "Hey, I better steer clear of this situation, because I might end up in prison." Hell no, he's thinking, "Let me at this dude . . ." When someone snaps, they're not thinking about the consequences of their actions, all they're thinking about is what they see, and what they're aiming for.

Everybody Suge rolled with tight in the Death Row camp thought like he did. They were thinking in the moment, not thinking about tomorrow. Tomorrow's the future and their attitude was to live for what was going on today.

I relate people to animals a lot. I was watching a television special the other night, and the subject was exotic pets. This guy had raised a lion, and when the lion was full grown, it eventually reverted back to what it is—a wild animal. I also saw the movie *Buddy* recently. This lady raised a gorilla from the time it was a baby. When the gorilla went back to its natural habitat, it attacked her.

If you have grown up in the hood all your life, that's the mind-set you have; you can try to get away from it, you can try to leave it, but it always comes back because you never forget where you're from.

It's easy for an outsider to misunderstand Suge and to question his actions. "He had everything, why couldn't he just be good and stay out of trouble?" That's like asking a pit bull to drop his guard and become a kitten. A pit bull can be the smartest, sweetest, most loving and loyal dog when it wants to be, but it'll never drop its guard, and if you challenge it, it'll fight till the death. That's who it is.

I honestly can't say how I'd behave if I were put to the test. I haven't been put in a situation where I would have to revert back to that mentality. If I were, I have not doubt I would. It's natural surviving instincts.

Suge Knight may have been guilty of believing in his own hype, but the biggest regret I have for Suge Knight is he could have made a difference. However, he had blinders on from left to right. He could only see straight ahead. If he could have seen the big picture, maybe he would have gotten off the path he was on. I have nothing but love for Suge Knight, and I hope when he gets out, he'll still have a leg up. I'm sure he'll never go broke. There is every reason to believe he's squirreled away enough money to live on. The point isn't money, though, it's whether or not he'll have taken time to analyze everything that's happened in his life and be able to clean his actions up.

Things had gotten so fucked-up toward the end, Tupac wasn't even allowed to take a cassette outside of the studio when he was working on tracks. He couldn't listen to his own music outside of the studio, because Suge wanted to own everything.

My hope for Suge is, he'll take the time in prison to become a bigger, better man. I know that man's already inside of him. During the year I knew Suge, I saw him do a lot of good things. He donated money to community youth centers, supplied Compton with Christmas turkeys and toys during the holidays. His Mother's Day parties were legendary. Over one thousand single moms would be invited to the events, including all the moms of the Death Row family, and he wasn't doing this to make a big show out of it. He seemed to be doing it from his heart.

You gotta understand, I knew some of the boys he rolled with, and these were guys who never had opportunities before Suge Knight made it. I'll never forget Heron, one of his closest homeboys. This dude was so cool, and we got along really well because Heron was yok'd, meaning he was a cut brotha like me. At Super Bowl XXX, we were kickin' it together. He'd gotten really into bodybuilding when he was in prison, and it was something we had in common. I'll never forget this fool telling me his philosophy on women. Heron was a good-looking man and knew he could have any women he wanted, but he was on a whole different tip.

"I go out and find the ugliest hood rat I can find, and then I make her fall in love with me," he said. "And I fall in love with her, too. I really do. I'll love this girl. Once it's hooked up, I'm gettin' paid."

I laughed at this crazy nigga, but his point was she'd take care of him, no matter what, and with no complications. I told you, the ghetto is all about surviving the game any way you can.

Heron was on television after Suge was put in jail; he was introduced by Fox News as a member of Compton's Mob Pirus. He got in the face of the camera and said, "This ain't no game . . . I work, I pay taxes, too. That's right. And this is what Suge taught me. I ain't never had a job before in my life before I started working for Suge . . . [I'd been] in and out of jail. Did a little bit of everything . . . Now, I'm a born-again worker."

Heron's dead now. You know why? After Suge was thrown in jail, a lot of his boys lost their jobs and went back to doing the only thing they knew how. They went back to the streets. Heron was found in his car, shot seventeen times, on the corner of Fairfax and Santa Fe.

Suge's suffered a lot of losses, Pac, Heron, his freedom. Suge must know if he wasn't in prison, Heron might still be alive. He might still have been working for Suge that day, and not been in the wrong place at the wrong time. The freedom that's been taken away from him, from the ladies he had, to his children, to the homies he used to party with, he's lost all of that.

Ironically the fight he was involved in at the MGM Grand was one of those fights that happened every day when you hung around Death Row. It was no more or less significant than any other incident that was just a daily occurrence of the Death Row entourage. Either someone came looking for trouble, or they were out for trouble. Didn't matter. It was just another day. For Suge to be locked up on something as petty as getting a few kicks in, is remarkable when you think about the other things that went down.

I'm not saying Suge's a saint. A lot of bad shit went down, there's no question. I couldn't believe the *L.A. Times* let him get away with comparing himself to our great leaders. It ends a sympathetic story on Suge with him saying: "Sometimes people get sacrificed when they try to stand up . . . Malcolm X, Martin Luther King."

Well, Suge Knight was no Malcolm X or Martin Luther King. In every interview he ever did for television or newspapers, he told what we called "cover-up talk." Suge did what he need to do. But think about this—where else is a man like Suge Knight going to go when he wants to start a business? He's not going to walk into a bank, and ask for a couple million dollars. They'd laugh in his face, he's from Compton, he had a rap sheet.

My point is, he did do good things, too. During the time I worked for him, I saw more good than bad. Like I said up front, the truth is complicated. Judge Stephen Czuleger, the Superior Court judge who sentenced Suge to eight years in prison, summed it up best: "You blew it," he told Suge. He was right.

I never got the chance to tell all the other members of Death Row family how I feel about them, so I'd like to take this opportunity to do so now:

Snoop, the Doggfather, you're just totally a cool cat. Cool as ice. I wish you well.

Daz, a very talented producer, I hope you make it.

Kurupt, you're a very talented rapper, a total natural. You need guidance.

Dr. Dre was a brother who made the right choice.

To Nate Dogg, the ex-Marine, I just wanna say Semper Fi, Always Faithful, hang in there.

The Outlaws, I miss you dearly. Tupac's soldiers are lost without Pac, and their hearts are broken. Yak's with Pac in heaven.

To Afeni, I'd like to say I share your pain over the loss of your son, I've lost your son, also. It's true I was responsible for him, and I hurt every time I think about the night they took your son, my friend. I pray and hope with all my heart that you truly know I had nothing but love for Pac, as you know he had for me.

I'll never forget the first time he introduced us to each other. He said, "Mom, this is Frank, my number one security." I miss the times we used to talk in the mornings at your house. You were always so kind to me, and I appreciate all the things you've done for me. Whenever we were driving over to your house, Pac would say, "If you're hungry, Mom will make something for us to eat," and that you did, often.

I want you to know, my mom also lost one of her sons recently, and I know and hear much about a mother's grief and pain from the loss of a son.

I feel that same pain for Tupac, Afeni.

CHAPTER TWENTY-TWO

TO PAC

I remember watching Elvis in a press conference once. He was wearing a blue jumpsuit with a big ol' belt and he's sitting at a long table, with his father beside him. The reporters asked him about his image. He told the reporters he didn't create the image of "The King," the media created the image. He was just the man who was living *their image*.

Tupac's life was parallel to that. He lived the image that people and the media had portrayed for him. He never could have lived the image down, and most of the time, when people looked at him, they were only seeing the image, not the man. The first time Tupac got into a fight as "Tupac Shakur, Rapper," he became "Tupac Shakur, the Controversial Rapper." Forget the fact he'd been fighting his whole life, getting the shit kicked out of him by neighborhood thugs until he got big enough and strong enough to fight back. Once he became famous, and they hyped him to be this celebrity thug, to some degree, he got off on it. His favorite movie was *Juice*, in which he played a street kid turned gangster. Tupac's life was already taking that path, and the movie role went straight to his head—there was no turning back. It's not like he didn't already know the character. He identified with him, and in some ways, he became him.

One of the most memorable images of Tupac Shakur was taken in New York, after he was shot up in the lobby of a recording studio in November 1994, in a botched robbery attempt he blamed on Biggie's Bad Boy camp. Someone took a picture of Pac being put into the ambulance—he's all taped up, and fucked-up looking. You can barely see his face, he's got so much tape on him, he looks like a mummy man. As he's going down, he mad-dogs the camera, looks directly into the lens, and you can see an arm coming up, and I swear to God, he's flashing the Westside sign. He didn't give a fuck.

People don't understand how a person can be both poet and warrior, but that's who Tupac Shakur was. The thing is, once this gangsta image is out there, you've got the people who love it, the politicians, who use it, and the police, who hate it. More accurately, they hated him, and he hated them back. They didn't have any love for him when he was a homeless kid, and they certainly didn't show any love for him when he grew into a defiant young man.

Even more than the anger he felt toward the police was the anger he directed toward the black politicians, who vocally positioned themselves against him. He lashed out at people like C. Delores Tucker, and any other black politician who had power and could help him. He felt they were Uncle Toms, straight up. They knew exactly where he came from, the misery that was his childhood, the misery that a lot of ghetto kids share, and he hated them for turning their backs on those kids. He considered himself someone who could still have used some help, but rather than extend a hand, they despised him and they used him. Through his music, he attacked them for what they are, complete and total sellouts. This was the serious shit people started seeing, and those on the street level saw Tupac was coming from his heart with the *real*. This is when he started selling millions of records, and it's also what made him dangerous.

So many people were afraid of Tupac, and I know this firsthand, because who did they come to? Me. Whenever somebody had a problem with him or something they wanted from him, they'd come to me and ask what I thought they should do. Most of the time, I'd tell them, the only person who can answer their questions was Tupac. Sometimes I'd try to help out. When we were on the movie set, screenwriters came out of the woodwork, asking if I could get their scripts to Pac. He was booked, and wasn't interested in signing up for new projects, but he actually read the scripts anyway.

More often than not, if you came to Tupac from your heart, he respected that. The sad thing is, he needed better representation. I don't think he ever had someone who cared about him during his entire career as an entertainer. He needed a good manager, who sought to represent him correctly and to help have a good influence on him. Nobody around him had the influence to clean up his image. Most of the people around him either didn't care or were happy to see him perpetuate the bad-boy image. It became clear to me, he was in need of help.

During the time I spent with him, I saw his attitude toward Suge change, from one of love to one of suspicion. Only one time did he ask me to leave the room when he spoke on the phone with Suge. Most of the time I heard what was going on, and toward the end, it did not look good. He told me he was having Death Row audited. I don't know how far along he got with it, but he suspected some fucked-up shit was going on with his money. That's why, when he died, Afeni was shocked to find out her million-dollar baby didn't have any money of his own. Suge held the purse strings, and while Tupac never went without, he wasn't in control, either.

I knew if his life had continued and he'd gone to work for Euphanasia, his own label and I went there with him, I could have helped his situation. He respected my voice and trusted me a great deal, and I know he would've have listened to me when I tried to offer him advice. There's no doubt, he would have made the ultimate decisions on his career moves, but I think I could have guided him to some degree. Remember, you couldn't tell Tupac shit, but that didn't mean he didn't need good advice or Pac wouldn't have listened.

The other day I was at my post-office box, and I ran into this girl who worked there, who I'd known in passing. She was getting ready to quit her job there, and we realized we might never see each other again, so we talked for a while. She finally asked me what I do for a living and I told her I was writing a book. She said, "For real? What do you write about?" I told her I was writing a book about my experiences as a bodyguard for Tupac Shakur.

She said, "I guess you weren't much of a bodyguard. He wasn't supposed to get killed."

I started to say something about how I was in a different car and wasn't allowed to have my gun strapped on me, and I realized there was nothing I could say, so I just made the conversation brief, wished her well and left.

It left me so depressed all day, and I couldn't shake it.

It happens all the time. I was invited to judge a bodybuilding competition in December, three months after Tupac died, and one of the other judges says to me, "Hey bodyguard, you didn't do such a good job, did you?" They were making jokes, and what can I say? I didn't find them very funny. "Some things are beyond our control," I told them, but it doesn't matter what I say. I realize the public perception of me is that I didn't do my job that night. It doesn't matter that for a year I was the best bodyguard anybody could hire. I was fiercely loyal, down for anything that came our way, and kept Tupac from getting in shit time and time again. Fuck it, there's nothing I could do or say to make people think differently about me. If I was working for the president of the United States and he'd gotten shot, it wouldn't have been any different. People would still look at me, like I didn't know how to do my job. To them, the circumstances are irrelevant. It's hard, though, to think that people I know, and people I'm friends with, hold these thoughts in their head, but I'm the kind of person who doesn't like excuses. Excuses are just like assholes, everyone has 'em and they all stink. That comes from my military training. There's no room for error and mistake. It happened, and it's something that I have to live with for the rest of my life.

I think about that night all the time. Either somebody asks me about what I'm doing, or someone makes a joke, and what can I do but go along with the joke?

Right now, I have the comfort of writing this book and knowing people with open hearts will understand what really went down that night.

The fucked thing is, I used to be so proud to say what I did for a living and who I did it for.

It makes me feel bad because I know Tupac trusted me, and I know I was worthy of his trust. There's so many times when I kept that boy from harm. I remember going to the Soul Train Awards in '96 and we were at his house off Wilshire and I asked him if he wanted me to roll with him in the Rolls-Royce they were driving to the show.

He said, "Hell no, I want you behind me, nigga. That way if niggas come out shooting, they'll know the bodyguards are behind us and you can get out and shoot back. Shit, we may get shot, but you can still shoot back." I remember him saying that back in March, and I've never forgotten it.

Lo and behold, it happened just like he thought it would happen, and what could I do? I couldn't get out and throw rocks. I ran to the car, and that's all I could do. Even as I look back now, and remember that arm coming out of the car, it shocked all of us, everyone had a delayed reaction that was in that car, and nobody was able to open the door faster than me.

But I replay that night in my head all the time and have never stopped thinking about it.

In my mind and then later on in my heart, I realized I'd let him down. I'm human, and I felt the repercussions of my own self-guilt for not being able to shoot back, to shoot someone. The question that coming back to me from that night and the next day is, "Why didn't you have your gun?" That was the main thing everyone wanted to know.

Then that turned into, "If you had your gun . . . you coulda done this, or you coulda done that."

Yeah, I could've hit some innocent bystander, who just happened to be out on the Strip that night, too, and what would that have resulted in? Me doing time.

But it fucking bothers me. It bothers me all the time. I talk to Tupac every day. Above my fireplace on the mantel, I have an altar to Tupac. It contains photos of him, and framed pictures of his Death Row photos and magazine covers. I look him in the eye and say, "I'm sorry. I wish I could've done something for you."

I had a really vivid dream the other night and when I woke up I remembered hearing Pac say to me, "I forgive you, Frank. It wasn't your fault."

I know it was him speaking to me from the grave, because I didn't have this dream right away, and knowing Pac, he wouldn't have accepted the situation right away.

Wherever Tupac is right now, he knows his death is weighing heavily on my heart and he must've felt it was the time to release me from my own pain. No one understands that pain except for me. Death Row got so tied up in Suge's situation, they never tried to come to me and say they understood what happened. It was easier to turn on me than to accept the fact the party was over. Even though I understand it now, at the time, I needed someone to care about me. I had suffered a loss, too.

I talked to Norris, who's running Death Row while Suge's in jail, and he was trying to get me to meet with David Kenner's investigator before Suge was sentenced, I asked him, where were they before they decided they needed me to testify? Norris listened to me and agreed, and said I was right, they did leave me high and dry after Pac's death, and he apologized.

You can apologize all day long, but how do they know it didn't fuck me up mentally?

Death Row was such a family, and if I was part of the family, why didn't they try to help me, too? An employer who sees an employee suffering is supposed to try to get that employee help, try to get him counseling. Snoop is the only one who made some effort to reach out to me after Pac's death. He had one of his bodyguards, Marcus, call me up to check on me and make sure I was holding up. He even told him to make sure to keep a close eye on me because he thought a circumstance like this could make somebody suicidal. That's a very real possibility and luckily for me, I'm a strong person, strong enough to keep myself intact.

But I am still human and I did still feel the effects of his death strongly, and the aftermath is what hit me the hardest. I know today I'm still not out of the woods. I still have to watch out that I don't stumble into depression and it's not easy. I've suffered a lot of losses in the past year. In many respects, I lost my family, which had been Death Row for the past year of my life.

Nothing in my life came close to the death I witnessed that night.

Before I worked for the company, I'd been forewarned about Death Row from people I knew in the music industry or fellow law-enforcement officers. I was told to be careful and warned about the trouble that followed Death Row around. It all went in one ear and out the other. I didn't care because I had no fear about Death Row. It was a job and I was getting paid; I had bragging rights and it was all fun.

A year later, it's a different story. I hesitate before I tell anybody anything about myself. I don't want to open up wounds that haven't finished healing.

I've had opportunities to bodyguard again, but it's too soon to determine if I'll ever bodyguard again. Kevin Hackie, who was my relief bodyguard with Pac, just got his license to run a security business and he asked me to work with him, and I told him I'd have to think about it. It's too soon to say if I could do it again. The thought of going out there and carrying a gun again and knowing I can never put that gun down for a second, scares me now.

Sometimes I trip back in time and think, What would've happened if

I had my piece on me that night in Vegas, and I shot everybody up in that car? Would I have been a hero again in the eyes of Death Row and everyone? Would I have shot the shooter? Ultimately, would it have mattered? Tupac would still be dead, and Lord knows where I would be.

When people say they wouldn't change anything in their lives, it's because they can't. It's not that they wouldn't. The reason you can't do anything differently, is we don't know what's in our future, we can't see our own future. We can only see the past, because we've already lived the future to see the past.

To look back and say, "I would've done this or that" is to say, "When I got out of high school, I would've gone to college." But I wouldn't have because it was my destiny to go into the service. It was my destiny to work for Death Row and to go through the steps and the stages I went through. I can't reverse those things.

I don't regret working for them, and I don't regret working for Tupac. I'll always have the memories we shared and that was part of my lifeline. My theory of life is we have this path we travel down and from the time we are born until the time we die, we're walking this path, this line, and everything that's on that path we're going to encounter, regardless. That's the way God planned it. It's our life.

You can't change the lifeline. People get mad and don't understand why things happen the way they do, but our lives are preplanned. We think we have control over our lives, and we do have control over what's right and wrong; if we know we're walking a path, we know we have choices to make a right or a wrong decision. We have the right to choose how to live.

The things that happened with Tupac, I don't regret any of it.

Things were meant to be, and you can rest assured Tupac had no fear of death. If you listen to all of his lyrics, you can hear his fearlessness. He looked at life, like, *Hey, I'm gonna go when it's time for me to go, and I know how I'm gonna go*. It was just a matter of time—it was gonna happen. It was his lifeline and his destiny.

I miss Tupac on a daily basis. I still feel a responsibility to him now. I want to show people who read this book the sides of him they may have known or may not have known. The man was actually at a point in his life where he was trying to change and come out and be different. It started with doing movies again. He wanted to start that slate clean. In his early films, he was late and was fucking up all the time. He had a bad reputation for being a good actor, but an actor who didn't give a fuck. At the time, he had more thug than business in him.

He was maturing in ways that only he knew, and a lot of people didn't see or didn't care to see. Pac was never late for *Gridlock'd*, on his own accord. It was a goal he'd set and he accomplished it. I remember getting into it with one of the producers. The driver was actually late a couple of times and Tupac pointed this out. Pac had moved and the driver didn't know how to get to his house so the driver showed up late. The producer apologized and everything turned out cool.

He wanted to set a better example all around. At one point, he even asked me to put him on a vitamin program and to set up a home gym at a spare room in his Wilshire house. He was determined to start taking better care of himself. He even asked me to train him. He wasn't giving up Thug Life, but he was changing. He was trying to tone it down. On a scale of one through ten, he went from being a high ten, to a five. He wasn't all the way there, but he was halfway.

He still flipped when pushed, though. This may seem to some people like he wasn't really changing, but he was. There were times when the Li'l Homies would get into it, and he stepped to it and tried to neutralize. On the production shoot for the videos of "Made Niggas" and "Hit 'Em Up," he tried to break up a fight Muta had gotten into. He wasn't in the middle of it, he was trying to slow it down.

Once again, though, the media hyped it up like Pac was instigating the shit. Just like at the Soul Train Awards. The reports read that Tupac had pulled a gun on a member of Biggie's entourage. That was a total lie, a member of Biggie's entourage pulled a gun on Pac. As long as they had something negative to say about Tupac, the media would blow it up. As far as the good things he did, you never heard about it. The media likes a bad boy, and I'm not saying he was an angel, I'm just saying they never gave the brotha a chance. Even when he wasn't being the Tupac of old, they turned him into it.

He didn't give a fuck, though. What could he do? He just went about his business, becoming more financially savvy. He started Euphanasia, his record label, *Makaveli*, he was helping foundations. You could see the changes. He was moving toward more positive things. He was still fighting within himself to change, it wasn't easy for him. Like a true Gemini, he was stuck between right and wrong. He was making good choices that had great meaning behind them, but there was always something ready to pull him back in. If it wasn't himself, it was the people he surrounded himself with.

It's like the old cartoon, with the devil on one shoulder and the angel on the other.

"Do it, do it, do it," says the devil.

"Don't do it, don't do it," says the angel.

That was Thug Life for Tupac. Always being down, hating anyone who's a sellout, who pretends shit still ain't wrong in the hood—but just the same, he was trying to do good. He was making enough money, and doing well for himself, and he wanted to make amends with his public. He wanted the future to be different for himself.

Imagine Pac if he had five more years. He would've been Dr. Dre's age, and my guess is he would've parted ways with Death Row and got on his own two feet. Tupac wasn't looking to get shot on September seventh and looking to die on September thirteen—that was not his plan. His plan was to make more money, make more movies, make more music, meet more women, smoke more weed, and be where he wanted to be: on top of his game.

Just like Michael Jordan is always on top of his game—he's the best basketball player—Tupac wanted to be on top of his game as the world's best rapper, which he was. He was well on his way.

But there was somebody way more powerful than anybody on this earth, who had different plans for Tupac. He was not gonna live to see thirty years old. The man was so talented and so intelligent, it was like he had premonitions of his death. When God knows he's got a child who is that strong-willed, he's not gonna leave him to continue on that path of destruction, so he took him back.

Tupac knew what was coming. He was going to die, and he was going to die the way he died. That doesn't excuse me from not being able to do one thing or another for him on that night, but the truth is, a lot of shit went down strange that day and my guess is, God knew what he was doing. God didn't have plans for me to be shooting my gun off on that night.

It's not easy when you tell the truth. The truth is messy and the truth hurts, but when you're speaking the truth about Tupac Shakur, it means it's also funny and sometimes crazy. He was a true ghetto warrior, someone to be proud of. He was a kid, like myself, who didn't have shit, who, through talent and hard work, climbed out of the ghetto. No matter how many setbacks he had or how many people wanted to keep him back, he kept climbing.

You gotta realize something about people from the hood—they relate to Tupac's music better than anybody. The reason is simple. There are other rappers writing lyrics, talking about the streets or whatever, but no one's believing them or maybe some people are, but they don't have the ear of all the people. A lot of rappers simply aren't rapping in a realistic way.

When Tupac wrote his lyrics, his stuff was for real, his music was real. It came from within himself, it wasn't fantasy. His raps tell the stories of his mother, his family, what he saw around him all the time. He came with lyrics from his heart that told stories people could relate to. Why do you think mothers loved that boy? Or women in general? Because Tupac was like everybody's son or brother or family member. He's that kid down the street that you worry about because you know he's having a tough time. That's why none of his real fans turned their back on Pac when he went to prison, because it would be like turning your back on your son.

That goes back to why he hated sellouts so much. A sellout, to Pac, was anybody who knows how fucked-up shit is on the street but who forgets about it. Who lets go of the thug, or tries to pretend the thug doesn't exist. To Pac, that's like turning your back on a kid who needs you. Yeah, that kid's fucked-up, but there's a reason he's fucked-up. *He* was that kid.

Regardless of how good or bad it's gonna be, if you can relate to the truth, you can relate to this book or you can relate to Tupac's rhymes. Tupac was kickin' it real, he didn't hide anything, and because of this, people relate to him. If Pac wanted to say, "Fuck the police" or "Fuck the world," he did. Other artists might be worried about their careers, and think it's gonna hurt them, so they wouldn't come that strong. There's only a couple other rappers out there, Ice T being one of them, who truly speak their mind and who aren't trippin' about what other people are going to think.

The people on the street want to know what's going on because it's happening in their neighborhood. He only rapped about things that were real. He didn't rap about things that were a maybe or a guess. Nothing was calculated or fiction. If you look at his songs, like "Dear Mama" or "If I Die Tonight," you know it's the real shit. It has something to do with some type of experience. "Dear Mama" was the song that crossed the line for women. If you think about a kid who has problems with his mom growing up, which Tupac obviously did with his mom, as he got older, he began to understand the hard time she had to go through and he had a fuller understanding of what it's like to be a mother in our society. He had respect now for not only his mom, but other women as well.

Even the way he rapped about God. You could hear him saying, *God, please forgive me for living the life I live here on earth, but in my heart I belong to you.*

A lot of the other guards who worked with Pac found it too stressful to be around him, but I liked his charisma and the aura he had about him. He was down to earth. I consider myself a very straightforward person; I'm not gonna lie about shit at my age, now. It's either you accept me the way I am and deal with it, or forget it. That's how he was.

I've always believed you can learn from people regardless of their age. I learn from everybody around me and never close my eyes to the fact someone could teach me something. At thirty-eight, I'm older than most of the people I was working with, but I didn't have any attitude about it. If there's something to be learned, I wanna learn it. If my daughter, who is ten years old, is gonna have an intelligent discussion with me, I'm going to listen to her because I might learn something.

That's the way I was with Pac. I watched him and observed him and learned. Tupac was an honest person, and he was a good person. He had a loving and forgiving heart. The sad thing is, I watched a lot of the rappers we worked with begin to turn around. Most of them didn't have father figures in their lives, and whether they knew it or not, they were looking for someone to give them some guidance.

In many respects, for Pac it was too late. He got into so many damn altercations the reality is, what went down on September 7 was inevitable. If he had dodged those bullets, he wouldn't have been out of the woods. Not until he made the decision to change his ways for life, would he have been able to see old age. Like many people who share a love for Tupac, I would have liked to see that happen, but it wasn't to be.

Before the night he was shot, he'd had a number of serious recent altercations. Recall the night Kevin Hackie drew his gun on the dudes after leaving a video shoot. That was only about two weeks before his death. We'd also had a number of problems on sets of videos, with homeboys fuckin' with him. Even on the days he wasn't looking for a fight, people were always testing him, and Pac just wasn't one to back down. It wasn't in his blood.

When he was in New York for the MTV Music Awards, he got into it with the rapper Nas and other New York artists in Central Park. He even got pissed at Snoop, because Snoop wouldn't have anything to do with it. He wasn't gonna go hang out in a New York park. By now it should be clear, if you're down with Pac, you've got to be *down* with Pac. This means 24-7, no questions asked. Snoop wasn't trying to be a gangsta, though.

Of course, the fight on September 7 is now etched in everyone's minds, but the truth is, Pac was getting into so many altercations, you couldn't keep up with him. If you add everything up, and factor in what went down on September 7, you're looking at a whole lot of angry people. A lot of people were trying to get at that man. What really happened, who really killed him, God knows and only God knows. Is it ever going to be solved? Probably not, unless some new shit comes up and somebody rats somebody out. Even then, you'd have to question their motives.

The truth is, Tupac couldn't even keep up with the shit surrounding him. Yes, he loved to fight, but the fights started coming too fast. It was all closing in on him, and the more I've thought about it, my faith and conviction in God makes me believe it was his time to go. For everything that was happening to that man's life and the madness surrounding him, God said, "You're coming home."

During the time I knew him, I watched him walk headfirst into every fire he could find, and it's almost as if he wanted to be burned. I truly believe Tupac Shakur wanted out of this world. I can't speak on his childhood, because I didn't know him then, I only know what's in his music and what I've read, but to know the man, is to know he suffered. Whatever pain he still carried with him was so deep, it often overcame him and he was ready to take on the world. In some metaphysical sense, all of his altercations turned into his death. When you figure how much he brought on himself, his behavior almost appears suicidal.

And yet he still shouldn't have gone out like he did. If we had had the proper security, and we were allowed to follow logical procedures—

with Suge's car flanked on all sides—Tupac wouldn't have been shot at that stoplight. If Reggie had arranged for us to carry our guns behind Nevada state lines, maybe things would have turned out differently. If Tupac would have listened to me and actually worn his bulletproof vest, perhaps he would be alive today.

If you read this far in the book, by now you know I don't like specu-lation. But if you want to know what I think happened that night, I'll tell you. I believe the shooters went to the club first, to see if we arrived. When they determined we hadn't arrived yet, they went back out onto the Strip to look for us. We were traveling with an entourage so it wasn't difficult to see us, and when we made that turn onto Flamingo and came to the red light at the next corner, that's when they saw their play, and that's when they did what they did. Obviously they were willing to die, too. There were so many cars, and knowing Death Row and knowing everybody affiliated with Death Row is going to be packin', that was a real gutsy move.

Do I think it was planned? No. I think it was directly related to the fight at the MGM Grand. It was the *"Menace II Society"* scenario. Just like in the film, a beat-down occurs, the guy goes and gets his homeboys, comes back and takes care of business. There's all this talk about the dude being friends with Puffy, and all this East Coast–West Coast drama. Whatever. All I know is, the shit was personal. I'm not saying I can finger anyone, but if I was a known gang member and I had a set and half my set was out there with me and I just got my ass kicked, I'm gonna go back, tell my boys, and we're gonna go do what we gotta do. Break 'em off something. That's the mentality. It's not a crazy hypothesis.

Ultimately Tupac didn't die in vain, he died because he was living too fast and living too angry, but the fact is, he might not have died that night if people weren't slippin'.

Now, I live with an indentation in my head, an everlasting imprint of that night. It's never going to go away. The people who were in the car with me have the exact same memory, and it's never going to leave our brains. We all saw the same thing, and we're all helpless. It never should have hap-pened, not on that night, not in that way.

Tupac's death touched everyone, from Wrightway and Death Row, to the media and to all of us who worked with him. I think about him every day, wondering what else I could have done for him, realizing there was nothing I could have done. I can't dwell on his death, because if I did, I'd be dwelling on a lot of others'. In November, my younger brother Curtis died of an overdose. He was only thirty-three years old; he was the third-youngest and the most quiet of all my mother's children. He never hurt anybody, and my mom loved him so much. My stepfather's son, my step-brother Adrian passed away. Adrian helped rescue me from Chicago when he moved me to Harvey, Illinois, in my teens. He died of lung cancer in May. An ex-girlfriend committed suicide, and another good friend died of pancreatic cancer.

And then, of course, there's Tupac. Tupac's death affected me the most because we'd been spending so much time together and because there were public reminders of his death everywhere I turned. I grieved and I grieved over the loss of that boy, we had such a strong connection. Perhaps it's my fault, but not once while working with him, did I think to myself, *Now, you know, Frank, this is a high-risk job, and there's a chance you might lose him.* He certainly had enough enemies where I probably should have thought about it. I didn't, though. He was just so full of life.

When Puffy wrote his tribute to Biggie, the single that Faith sings on, "I'll Be Missing You," he couldn't have known the effect it was going to have on me. When it debuted on MTV, I recorded it, and I watched as he opened the video by telling viewers, "The song goes out to everyone who's lost a loved one." I looked up at the picture of Pac above my fireplace, and he was staring right at me, and I just started trippin'. I started thinking about everybody I'd lost over the past year, and all this emotion began flooding out of me. *Oh no*, I said to myself, *not now*—but I couldn't stop it. I just freaked out. I think it was the first time the weight of all the losses I'd suffered hit me, and I just let it out. I let it all out. I must have watched that video five times that night. How ironic it seems, that it was written for someone Tupac considered his enemy. How ironic they are both dead.

It was a catalyst for me, though, to move back in time, and I remembered this little boy we'd met the very first day we showed up to film *Gridlock'd*. He was with two li'l homies, and he was standing behind a fence. Pac's trailer was parked on the other side of the fence, and I don't know if they knew whose trailer was parked there, but when this little boy saw him, he shouted, "Hey, it's Tupac!"

Pac walked over to the fence where he was standing, and he started talking to the li'l guy. The boy started singing, *"I wanna be your N-I-G-G-A, we can drink liquor and smoke weed all day . . ."*

Pac stopped him and said, "No, no, no, no. . . . That's not the version for you guys. Y'all not supposed to be singing it like that. You're supposed to be singing the clean version. I don't want you repeating the nasty version, if you're gonna repeat my words, go buy the clean stuff—you guys are too little to be singing those words."

The boy said, "Fuck that, Pac. We *down*. We Westside."

Pac looked at him and started shaking his head. He was buggin', but he started preaching to the boy. "No, no, no—you guys can't be doing that. Y'all walking around singing the dirty lyrics, and people are gonna get mad at me because we got li'l kids doing it. I record the clean stuff for y'all. That's what you supposed to be singing."

It fucked with him. He loved kids, and he wasn't wanting to hear that. He was the first to say he didn't want to be anybody's role model, but he knew his fame had turned him into just that. The truth is, kids who've grown up in the hood don't have much of a childhood to begin with, and, for better or worse, they relate to the words he raps.

When I started working on this project, I called Larry to help me remember the pieces of my childhood—I was only remembering fragments. Larry told me the reason I had so much trouble remembering it is, we didn't have a childhood. I realized I'd spent most of my adult life trying to forget it. I think Tupac had done the same.

I listen to the radio and all the reports on the Internet about people believing Tupac is still alive. I want to lay those rumors to rest. Tupac Shakur died on September 13, and Detective Becker was a witness to the autopsy, which took place on September 14. When the coroner was finished, they asked Afeni what she wanted to do with the body and she told them to cremate it. I found out about it because one of the guards who was with us at the hospital, who's a member of the LAPD named Rich—he was the guy who wouldn't go to Italy because Reggie wasn't paying us enough—he was in charge of picking up the ashes from the coroner's office. He hand-delivered the ashes to Afeni on Sunday morning, September 15.

If Tupac comes back, I'll be the first one to bow down. But we're gonna have to wait until the next lifetime.

*   *   *

When I first saw the scar the doctors left behind after they had removed his lung, I knew in my heart Thug Life was over. The scar cut a line between *Thug* and *Life*—the tattoo he wore proudly on his chest—and to me, it symbolized the end. I believe his mother already knew the same thing, that Tupac was probably gone. He was probably hovering over us, looking at himself and giving his mother the signal saying, *I don't want to come back to this. Disconnect me. I'll be much happier.*

Everything he ever sang about was death. He always believed in a place that was better than Earth. He strongly believed he wasn't going to live to see thirty. He was shocked he made it to his twenty-fifth birthday. He knew he was going to die and he knew how he was going to die. The lifestyle he was living made it pretty obvious. He didn't give a fuck. He'd already made his peace with God, and he was ready to go at any time.

I understand this very well, because I'm ready for death. There's a lot of times I get tired of this world we live in, and thoughts of suicide have filled my head. But I think about my mother, and I saw what my brother's death did to her, and I think about my daughter, and I know I need to be there for her.

But I strongly believe in God, and I know Tupac also had a strong belief in God, and he's in a better place.

There's a possibility that Tupac's shooter is reading this book, and to him I want to say, There's no such thing as a perfect crime. You may have gotten away with it so far, but your judgment day will come. You may be hiding now, but the Father, whose eyes never close watched what you've done to one of His sons, and his life was not for you to take. Therefore, come Judgment Day, you will be judged, and your soul will be taken and never given back.

Until then, I hope you don't sleep well at night.

CHAPTER TWENTY-THREE

EULOGY

I'll always remember the night they took my homeboy. I try to block it out but it replays again and again in my mind. Now, in my heart is where I'll keep Tupac, and now half my heart is filled with death. To those who share that half, rest in peace: my father, my two brothers, my girlfriend, my friends, I'll always miss each of you—Perry, Curtis, Adrian, Diane, David, and Tupac, the voice of our generation. If there's one thing I want all his fans to know, it is this: Tupac had a truly loving heart. No matter what you hear or what you read, believe me when I tell you his heart was filled with love. I know why so many of you want to believe he's still alive in this world, you're all hoping to hear from him again. The truth is, he's in a better place—a place where he has found peace and his heart is trouble-free.

This book is dedicated to the memory of Tupac Shakur.

Before I end this last page, I'd like to lift my hat for one final salute to that young brave black brotha.

Rest in peace, Tupac, I miss you.

One Love.